the new exotic garden

the new exotic garden

Will Giles

MITCHELL BEAZLEY

*A very special thanks must go to my long-time friend
and mentor Sandra Pond for the artwork in the
gardening techniques section, for burning the candle
at both ends, and for her patience with me whilst
I was writing this book.*

THE NEW EXOTIC GARDEN
by Will Giles

First published in 2000
by Mitchell Beazley, an imprint of
Octopus Publishing Group Ltd,
2–4 Heron Quays,
London E14 4JP

ISBN 1-84000-241-7

A CIP catalogue copy of this
book is available from the British Library

Executive Editor **Alison Starling**
Executive Art Editor **Vivienne Brar**
Senior Editor **Michèle Byam**
Designers **Lisa Tai, Helen Taylor**
and **Vicky Short**
Production **Karen Farquhar**
Picture Research **Claire Gouldstone**
Indexer **Hilary Bird**
Illustrations **Sandra Pond**

Half-title page: *Agave parryi.*
Title-page: Containers, cordyline, datura, and a standard
bay in the author's garden in Norwich, England.
Contents page: An *Echeveria* species above
Arctotis x *hybrida* 'Flame'.

Set in Gill Sans

Printed and bound in China by
Toppan Printing Company Limited

contents

What could be more intriguing than expecting to see a small suburban garden and instead finding, hidden away, an area of such luxuriant tropical growth that the plants tower above you, as in a tropical glasshouse without a roof. Once virtually unknown, gardens like these are increasingly found in cities, suburbs, and country areas throughout the northern hemisphere. They belong to gardeners who have found that, whatever the size of their gardens, they have been able to create exotic fantasies of their own.

This book is intended for those gardeners who are tired of the usual style of borders and plants, and who wish for something more exhilarating and fulfilling with a sense of fantasy and intrigue. Even those who live in regions where frosts are likely during the winter months can steal a bit of tropical magic. Exotic gardening does not have to consist entirely of tender plants; it can also include hardier species that originated in the cooler areas of the tropics, such as the mountainous areas of Kenya or Mexico, as well as plants that may give the impression of being exotic but are not native either to the tropics or to hot dry regions.

In Europe, the fascination with tropical plants began more than two hundred years ago and reached a peak during the mid-19th century, when practically every major capital, however cold, managed to put on a display of the exotic plants brought back from newly discovered lands. Many of them were housed in glass houses and in domed glass cases – known as wardian cases – to protect them from northern winters.

In Britain, the development of the glasshouse was a result of the repeal in 1845 of the British glass tax, together with the production of reasonably priced good-quality glass. In mainland Europe, new glass houses displayed collections of ferns, palms, bromeliads, orchids, and other exotica. Their designers made imaginative use of pathways, rock features, waterfalls, and great gantries that visitors could walk along to view the plants from above. These highly colourful plants with exotic flowers and leaf patterns must have seemed amazing to the public of the time.

ABOVE *The conspicuously red-stemmed Canna 'Striata', like all cannas, is native to tropical and sub-tropical America. The tuberous roots were once eaten by the native peoples of Colombia and Ecuador. Cannas were first grown as subtropical bedding plants at a temperate latitude by a M. Année in Chile in 1846.*

RIGHT *The majestic Abyssinian or Ethiopian banana, Ensete ventricosum 'Maurelii', is an exceedingly fast-growing perennial that reaches its full height in only a few years. It is an absolute show-stopper in the garden. To the left of the banana is the tall, flowing grass Miscanthus sacchariflorus.*

By the mid-19th century a garden fashion for both inside and outside planting was well under way. With an ever increasing variety of plants becoming available, public interest in the exotic began to grow. They were grown in the new hothouses, or stove houses, as they were called (larger structures were sometimes referred to as winter gardens). The glass was cheap, labour was cheap, and heating was cheap, so no expense was spared in keeping the temperature up as high as necessary – a minimum temperature of 21°C (70°F) was quite normal. This produced a damp, humid, lush atmosphere, which the plants absolutely revelled in.

One of the earliest Victorian proponents of the new style of bedding was John Gibson, who produced large foliage displays in Battersea Park, London. As well as the more familiar bedding plants, he used exotica such as bananas and tree ferns. Another well-known Victorian plantsman, William Robinson, had a dislike of formal and regimented gardens, and in his book *The Subtropical Garden* (1871) he wrote about many subtropical and tropical plants that could be planted out during the summer months. Robinson maintained not only that a subtropical style of garden could be created using hardy plants that had an exotic look, but also that only exotic plants that actually thrived outside should be grown, rather than those that would sit unhappily in the soil with cold roots.

ABOVE *The dark foliage and red flowers of* Lobelia cardinalis *interplanted with* Canna 'Striata'. *Beneath them is the red-flowered* Dahlia 'Bednall Beauty', *while to the right is* Solenostemon 'Lemon Dash'.

RIGHT Solenostemon scutellarioides (syn. Coleus blumei) *is a useful plant that can be grown as an annual for instant colour. It is available in many colour combinations and patterns.*

FAR RIGHT *A demonstration of how you can successfully grow houseplants outside during the summer. An underplanting of* Calathea makoyana *acts as a foil for the darker leaves of* Colocasia esculenta *(above) and* Caladium bicolor 'John Peed'. *The fern* Pteris cretica *var.* albolineata *grows happily among these exotics (top left).*

THE NEW EXOTICISM

Gardeners soon discovered that many of the plants recommended by experts such as Robinson would not only survive outside during a British summer but would actually thrive – especially if the more tender species and varieties were put under glass for the winter months. They also learned that most exotic species had much longer flowering periods than the more traditional cottage-garden plants of temperate climates.

By the end of the 19th century the popular fashion for bedding had started to wane. Gardeners such as Gertrude Jekyll were extolling the virtues of the cottage garden, so the use of exotic bedding declined, and with the loss of the large estates, and the patrons who used to pay for them, the fashion for exotica came to an end. Large glass houses were now too expensive to maintain, so the opportunity to overwinter plants had virtually disappeared. In addition, labour, so necessary for the maintenance of glass houses, was no longer cheap.

In recent years, however, the desire for growing exotica has returned, especially in the form of hardier planting that look tropical. This was partly due to the boom in the travel industry from the 1960s, which enabled many more people to fly to tropical, far-flung places fairly cheaply. Like me, many returned to their own countries wanting to grow some of the exotic species they had seen on their travels.

My own exotic gardening career began when, in 1982, I purchased half an acre of land (0.2023 ha) that had not been touched for over 30 years. It was covered in sycamore trees, brambles, bindweed, old tin baths, rusty bicycles, and a few other things I would rather not mention. I had no idea at the time that the garden would change into the exotic paradise it is today. However, it was probably fortunate that the land was so overgrown, because it gave me the chance to start from scratch.

RIGHT *In a quiet, cool, and moist area of the author's garden, multi-coloured* Ipomoea lobata *scrambles up the stem of a standard and variegated* brugmansia. Tulbaghia *species, members of the lily family, flower in the foreground.*

LEFT *This striking close-up of a single* Canna 'Durban' *leaf illustrates just how exquisite the patterns on the leaves of subtropical plants can be. Although grown primarily for their beautiful foliage, cannas also produce richly coloured flowers.*

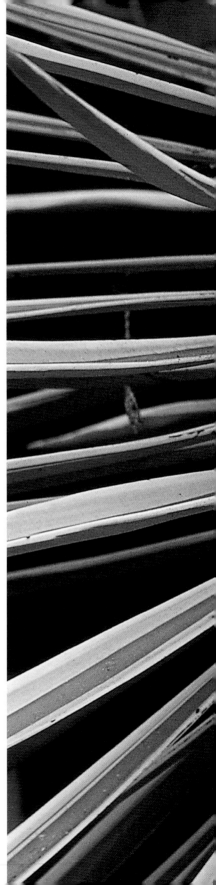

LEFT *Plants of varying colours, shapes, and textures have been successfully combined in this exotic border by being bedded in the ground already planted in containers. An old birdbath contains the fragrant succulent* Aeonium balsamiferum, *while a standard bay tree is set in an old orange pot. Bedded plants include a brugmansia, the banana* Ensete ventricosum 'Maurelii', *pittosporum, and* Dahlia 'Bednall Beauty'.

RIGHT *Nature always takes its own path, as demonstrated here by the way in which the nasturtium* Tropaeolum majus 'Hermine Grashoff' *winds its way through the stiff leaves of a large variegated yucca, making a stunning contrast in both colour and form.*

For the first eight years or so I spent all of my spare time clearing the garden, and planting fairly common herbaceous plants in the spaces. Then, in the mid 1980s, I went on a series of trips that took me to India, parts of Africa, and North and South America. On my return I began to plant a few more exotic species to try to emulate the feel of the tropical places I had seen. My problem at the time was lack of money and information, as well as the non-availability of many plants I wanted to grow.

In 1988, Myles Challis published a book, *The Exotic Garden*, which became a kind of garden bible to exoticists in Britain. Nothing of distinction had been written on the subject since the Victorian era, and Challis's book was completely inspirational to would-be exotic gardeners. Nowadays the situation is completely different, as there are far more purveyors of exotica in Europe and elsewhere in the world, many of them accessible through the Internet. Among the plants that are now more commonplace are the aroids, bananas, and palms, to name but a few. Other easily obtainable exotic plants from warmer climes include arctotis from South Africa, aeoniums from Madeira, the Mediterranean, and North Africa, and lobelias, salvias, and verbenas from Mexico.

LEFT *A shingle path in the author's garden is thickly planted on either side with exotics that include the spotted laurel,* Aucuba japonica *(far left).* Cordyline australis *'Atropurpurea', planted in a ribbed pot, is overshadowed by the Chusan palm,* Trachycarpus fortunei. *The grey, felted leaves of the evergreen shrub* Plectranthus argentatus *lie beneath the billowing, black-stemmed bamboo* Phyllostachys nigra *(centre).*

ABOVE *The magnificent, golden-yellow culms of a young* Phyllostachys vivax *'Aureocaulis'. The tidy habit and sparse leaves show off the thick culms with maximum impact. With age, the culms becomes randomly striped with green. This must be one of the most stunning of all bamboos.*

For the novice exotic gardener, the new availability of exotic plants presents the problem of what to grow. Many of the visitors to my garden, seeing that I have planted out various houseplants, have the impression that absolutely any plant can be grown outside. However, in reality, plants will only thrive if you provide the right conditions. I am especially fortunate because my garden is on a south-facing hillside that drops 9m (30ft) from back to front. It also has very tall trees to the north, west, and east, which provide me with my own microclimate. Another advantage I have is that the soil in the garden is very free-draining, a necessity for overwintering plants that dislike having wet roots. If kept fairly dry during the winter, plants can tolerate much colder conditions.

The main thing when choosing plants is to be aware of the conditions that prevail not just in your garden but also in your local area. For example, if you live in a very windswept region I would suggest that you do not attempt to grow tree ferns but instead choose shrubs or small trees that will tolerate high winds. Similarly, if you live in a coastal area you will find that this type of microclimate is actually more favourable to exotic

plants because there tends to be little frost, especially along the coastline. Look around your own area to see which plants prefer drier, more windswept conditions. Alternatively, if you have the time and the room in your garden, a shelter-belt of trees makes a massive difference because it creates its own microclimate.

Above all, remember that the key to successful exotic gardening is to keep on experimenting with your planting. With this style of gardening there are no rules, no right or wrong way. If your particular fantasy is to grow a garden of palm trees and nothing else, don't be intimidated, go right ahead and indulge yourself. There will always be someone who will tell you that something will not work, or cannot be done. My philosophy is to do it and find out for yourself whether it works.

Usually you'll find that with just a little thought you can create an absolutely luscious garden with a mixture of hardy plants that look truly exotic, including plants that are not really exotic at all. For instance, last summer I planted out bromeliads, tillandsias, alocasias, and the like, all of which do well for me at this time of year. *Solenostemon (Coleus)* are no different from, certainly no less hardy than, petunias. If a particular scheme doesn't work then I'll know not to use those plants again.

There are so many interesting exotic plants out there; just try growing them and see what happens!

RIGHT *The entrance to this lush garden is guarded by three Chinese statues, representing Youth, Middle Age, and Old Age. Temples, pavilions, and latticed passageways among the luxuriant planting create the effect of a magnificent jungle ruin. The garden was created out of a raw swathe of the Beverly Hills Canyon in California.*

ABOVE LEFT AND LEFT *The spiky red seedheads and dark-bronze foliage belong to the evergreen Ricinus communis 'Carmencita'. In frost-prone areas, this luxurious and fast-growing perennial is best treated as an annual, making a large and stunning plant in one season. It was a favourite of Victorian gardeners for filling the backs of large displays of subtropical plantings, and is at its best when planted in a thicket. All parts of this plant, especially the seeds, are poisonous when ingested.*

Agave victoriae-reginae was discovered in 1875 in northern Mexico, and was named after Queen Victoria. Because of the beauty of the compact, variegated rosettes it also has the common name 'queen of agaves'.

In the design of an exotic garden the plantings can be divided into two groups, hard and soft. The hard plantings are made up of woody species, which are characteristically stiff, scaly, spiky, rigid, or erect, and tend to be more hardy. They are the backbone of the garden and will take you through the bleaker winter months. The soft plantings are the fleshier, and more delicate, species – although some of them are actually quite tough – and are often feathery, trailing, arching, or velvety textured. They include many of the exotics that people think of as houseplants. In the exotic garden, both hard and soft planting is needed in order to maintain a balance in form and texture, and to prevent the garden from becoming boring and predictable.

For hard, permanent planting, use plants such as palms, bamboos, vibernums, New Zealand flax (*Phormium tenax*), and *Magnolia grandiflora* 'Goliath'. The latter, like the flax, is winter hardy, especially if planted against a south-facing wall. It is valuable too for its glossy, dark-green foliage, which is brown-felted on the underside.

For a softer effect, try one of the mainstays of the exotic garden, the Japanese banana, *Musa basjoo*. It is relatively hardy in temperate climes, but needs winter protection when planted permanently in the garden (*see pp. 98–99*).

LEFT *A section of a frond from the tree fern* Dicksonia antarctica. *The exquisite, lacy leaves are oblong to rhomboidal in outline, and the leaf petiols are covered in thick, cinnamon-coloured hairs. The two- or three-pinnate fronds can reach 2–3m (6–10ft) in length in milder climates. This plant, whose common name is the woolly tree fern, is an evergreen.*

RIGHT *The Japanese banana,* Musa basjoo, *has been growing in the author's garden for nearly a decade, and is now considerably multi-stemmed. Smaller exotics to be seen include* Canna 'Striata', Lobelia cardinalis, *and* Lysimachia 'Firecracker'. *To the right, in a pot, is a Canary Island date palm,* Phoenix canariensis, *next to a clump of tall* Kniphofia 'Royal Standard'.

When considering form you will need to strike a balance between the larger plants and the smaller ones used as underplantings. It is also essential to have a sculptural framework for your planting, using species with strong architectural shapes and interesting textures. Among the larger plants, forms can range from the arching leaves of the Japanese banana, *Musa basjoo,* to the equally large, clump-forming New Zealand flax (*Phormium tenax*), with its sword-like leaves, and spikes of red-purple flowers.

Smaller, hardy exotic plants worth growing for their forms include the wild ginger, *Asarum europaeum,* with its glossy, rounded leaves. This evergreen perennial is especially stunning when grown in the dappled shade of taller plants. *Arum italicum* subsp. *italicum* 'Marmoratum' is another shade-loving plant and has dark-green, arrow-shaped leaves with pale-green or white veining. The leaves last from winter to late spring, and are followed in summer by white spathes, and in autumn by spikes of orange-red berries.

For pure architectural form there is nothing quite like the ferns. With their finely formed, almost lacy, feathery leaves they provide texture as well as form. They are an amazing family of plants, ranging from the diminutive species that cling to rock-faces to large ones such as the woolly tree fern, *Dicksonia antarctica*, from Australia. This tree fern has a stout, fibrous trunk up to 6m (20ft) tall, and massive fronds up to 3m (10ft) long that form a spreading, evergreen canopy. In order to thrive it must be grown in a moist situation in dappled shade.

A complete contrast to the woolly tree fern is the common polypody, *Polypodium vulgare* 'Cornubiense', an attractive species of fern which has fresh-green, sculptural fronds 40cm (16in) long.

Like the ferns, the palms are absolutely essential in a garden for their exotic looks and strong architectural shapes. The most well known and robust members of this family must be *Trachycarpus fortunei*, which has a strong vertical stem and large, leathery fan-like leaves. The smaller European fan palm, *Chamaerops humilis*, is equally desirable. Initially it looks similar to *Trachycarpus*, although it is shorter, but with time it becomes multi-truncated and forms more of a domed shape. Palms prefer to be protected from prevailing winds, especially in the winter months. You have to try to simulate tranquillity for these plants.

Although many people think of cacti as plants for the glasshouse – where they look great to the avid collector but can be boring if placed in serried ranks – they always look wonderful when grown in pots outside. Both cacti and succulents seem to have an air of permanence that other plants lack.

Aeonium tabuliforme, *native to Tenerife in the Canary Islands, grows in an amazing geometric pattern. At this magnification it is possible to see the fine hairs that surround each individual leaf tip. This, the flattest of the aeoniums, is roughly the size of a dinner plate, with rosettes 50cm (20in) across.*

Cacti and succulents epitomize texture and form. The many different species of aloes are soft and spiky. They need well-drained soil, and must be south-facing; the majority must have full sun or they will become etiolated. In temperate climates, they are better grown in raised beds.

A plant that thrives in similar conditions to the aloe is the succulent *Aeonium* 'Zwartkop'. In its native habitat, in the Canary Islands, it grows in quite rough, stony ground. This is a wonderful species with such luscious, fleshy leaves that it almost looks edible. The more sun this plant receives, the blacker it gets; in really hot climates it becomes jet black.

The dramatic agaves from the New World have rigid, fleshy leaves with viciously-toothed margins and sharp, needle-like tips. *Agave americana* is grey-green and can reach 2m (6ft) in hot climates, but much less in cooler regions. *A. a.* 'Marginata', another large variety, has yellow-margined leaves.

Cacti and succulents offer an amazing variety of shapes, textures, and sizes, from globes to verticals, small to extremely large. *Echinocactus grusonii*, the golden barrel cactus, comes from the deserts of northern Mexico. In cooler, temperate regions it reaches 13–15cm (5–6in) across, but in the wild it will grow to a diameter of 60–90cm (2–3ft).

A contrast to the spiky succulent plants are those that have big leaves. One of the best for producing seemingly instant large leaves is the *Canna* – or Indian shot, as it used to be called, because its seeds look like pellets from a shot gun. Cannas are native to South and Central America, where they grow in moist areas, and along the margins of streams. They are very variable: many have green foliage, others have bronze-purple foliage and a few are variegated. One in particular, *Canna* 'Striata', has green leaves with prominent yellow striations and reddish stems which, in midsummer – depending on its situation – can rocket to a great height. This is a feature of cannas and other tropical plants in general; they are very fast growing compared with the relatively slow growth of indigenous temperate plants.

With their thrusting, upright stems, cannas not only make a strong statement but are also good companions for other plants, such as the softer-leaved *Solenostemon* (syn. *Coleus*) or the feathery *Cyperus papyrus*. *Verbena bonariensis* also has a good form, with long stems topped with tiny purple flowers. Although it grows to 2m (6ft), the slender stems allow you to see through to the other plantings behind, so it can be planted anywhere. It is also tolerant of high winds as the stems are fibrous and strong.

ABOVE *Euphorbias and an aloe set the scene in this planting of drought-resistant plants at the Huntington Botanical Gardens in California. This desert garden has around 2500 species of dry-land plant, co-existing in rambling beds edged with volcanic tufa rock.*

RIGHT *The Chusan palm, Trachycarpus fortunei, (centre) is surrounded by other exotic plants in the garden created by Myles Challis, one of Britain's leading exoticists. Amazingly, the jungle garden occupies an area that is only 6 x 12m (20 x 40ft), demonstrating how little space matters in exotic gardening.*

Bamboos are fantastic plants for the exotic garden, and there are so many different forms, sizes, and shapes. They range from the very small, around 60cm (24in), to the exceedingly tall, at 6–9m (20–30ft). They vary too in colour, thickness, and texture. For example, the culms (canes) of *Phyllostachys nigra* start off green, then gradually turn a burnished black. The forms they take depend on the way you grow them: you can allow them to make a nice tight clump, creating a really good focal point, or you can thin the stems out in spring so that the plant produces much bigger culms up to 2.5cm (1in) wide and 6m (20ft) tall (see p. 102).

The bamboos are a vast family containing elegant plants that can be small and clump-forming or invasive, so there are bamboos for every size of garden. In a very small garden or courtyard they can be grown in containers and pots, especially some of the Oriental glazed containers now readily available. Bamboos produce canes as short as 45cm (18in), such as those of the diminutive and bushy *Pleioblastus pygmaeus*, and as tall as 8m (25ft), as exemplified by the timber bamboo, *Phyllostachys bambusoides*, which is noted for its very thick canes. Some members of the grass family, such as the giant reed, *Arundo donax*, are bamboo-like in appearance. This tall, majestic grass grows up to 5m (15ft) and has alternate, arching, ribbon-like, mid-green leaves.

Pleioblastus auricomus (syn. *Arundinaria viridistriata*) is one of the smaller bamboos, growing up to 1.5m (5ft) in my garden. It should be treated like a herbaceous perennial, and cut down in spring to get fresh new growth. It has bright yellow leaves with green stripes, and is excellent planted in a shady or semi-shady position so that you have pools of yellow in hidden corners. Both this plant and another evergreen bamboo, *Fargesia murieliae*, are good for small gardens. The latter has small leaves on arching stems, and can grow to 4m (12ft), although it may only reach 1.5m (5ft), depending on the conditions. It is not inclined to spread very much, but the species *Sasa palmata* is very invasive. I have restricted it by planting it near a wall. *S. palmata* grows to 1.8m (6ft), with leaves 5cm (2in) wide and 20cm (8in) long. It will give any garden a very exotic, jungle-like feeling, especially after rain.

PREVIOUS PAGES *The European, or dwarf, fan palm,* Chamaerops humilis, *has dense, pinnate leaves with long, thin leaflets. This palm is often found growing on Mediterranean hillsides, where it can endure cold temperatures in winter. In such situations it often has a single trunk, although in cultivation it usually forms more than one.*

ABOVE *Three distinct types of planting illustrate how much variety can be achieved by contrasting form and texture.* Pleioblastus auricomus, *an excellent bamboo for the front of the border, grows between a clump of the silver-leaved evergreen* Astelia chathamica *and one of the many colourful varieties of* Solenostemon.

RIGHT *A fine stand of* Phyllostachys bambusoides, *the giant timber bamboo, growing at the Orto Botanico in Pisa, Italy. In its native eastern and central China the plant can reach a height of 20m (65ft), with the culms as much as 12–15cm (5–6in) in diameter, but when grown almost anywhere else it usually attains less than half this size.*

Bamboos provide movement and sound in the garden, as the canes wave and clatter in the wind. Grasses also have this effect, and some, such as *Miscanthus sacchariflorus*, are rather bamboo-like in form, although they produce new shoots annually. This grass is a good one to grow for its rustling effect if you don't want to grow bamboo.

Climbers that provide form and texture include the lovely trumpet vine, *Campsis radicans*, with vivid orange trumpets about 8cm (3in) long. It is a very subtropical-looking plant for growing on a south-facing wall, as is the passion flower, *Passiflora*, the hardiest of these being *P. caerulea*, the blue passion flower. Other good exotic climbers include *Solanum crispum* 'Glasnevin', *Solanum jasminoides* 'Album', *Vitis coignetiae*, and *Aristolochia macrophylla*, Dutchman's pipe, which has very odd-looking flowers. *Akebia quinata* flowers early, with small, bell-shaped, three-petalled flowers. In my opinion it is essential for the garden, although it cannot really be classed as an exotic. *Clematis armandii* is another essential, and is one of the few evergreen climbers. It has dark, glossy leaves, and in spring is covered with white flowers with a delicate scent. Because it needs protection from cold winds it is best grown in a sheltered courtyard.

This closely planted and very colourful exotic garden was created by Christopher Lloyd at Great Dixter. A group of the orange Dahlia 'David Howard' brightens the centre.

exotic colour

The exotic gardener's palette covers a complete colour spectrum, ranging from pale to an explosion of rainbow hues. Adventurous use of colour is the key to successful exotic planting – be bold, experiment, and try to forget traditional ideas of gardening good taste.

Experimenting with colour means finding out what you like, and not worrying about clashes. Pink and orange, orange and purple, can look wonderful together – there are no restrictions with this style of gardening. In the exotic garden, colours tend to be brash, very intense, and invariably bright. To get this effect make use of hybridized plants, which for the most part are more colourful than the species. However, it is also possible to be much more subtle in an exotic garden, and use only a few splashes of colour or just white among the myriad shades of green.

I tend to use yellows and reds, with a bit of purple, but you can have any colour combination you wish, or concentrate on just one colour in various shades. Colour, of course, comes from leaves, stems, bark and fruit, as well as flowers. For example, *Colocasia* 'Black Magic' has green juvenile leaves with purple veining, but as the leaves mature they gradually become darker and darker. It looks beautiful with red fuchsias dangling onto the black leaves; the colours really work well together.

ABOVE *The fabulously dark-leaved* Colocasia esculenta 'Black Magic' *dominates this group. The stiff, vertical, and variegated leaves are those of mother-in-law's tongue,* Sansevieria trifasciata 'Laurentii'. Impatiens *New Guinea Group, and, at the back, a* Solenostemon *hybrid provide additional exuberant colour.*

RIGHT *The vibrantly red-flowered and purple-leaved* Lobelia cardinalis *thrusts its way up between the green and yellow leaves of the striped* Canna 'Striata', *and the pink and purple leaves of* Canna 'Durban'. *Behind them are the yellow flowers of the purple-leaved* Lysimachia 'Firecracker' *and (on the right) a* Kniphofia *species.*

RIGHT *Raindrops splashed onto the petals of Canna 'Taroudant' magnify their vibrant colour. This canna is a modern variety, first raised in France. It has narrow green leaves and grows to a height of 1m (3ft). As one of the relatively small varieties of canna it is more suitable for the front of a border.*

LEFT Tropaeolum majus *'Hermine Grashoff'* is one of several double-flowering varieties of nasturtium. T.m. *'Darjeeling Gold'* is a similar variety, with bright lemon-yellow flowers. These nasturtiums can only be propagated by stem-tip cuttings. Like others in the genus, they are excellent for growing in gravel beds, as they thrive in poor soil.

BELOW *Exquisite but fleeting, the individual flowers of* Hemerocallis *species last only a day, although blooms are produced over several weeks. The yellow-orange variety* H. *'Burning Daylight', shown here, sometimes has a crimson flush.*

Black foliage is also attractive when planted with the giant reed, *Arundo donax*. *A.d.* 'Variegata', green with whitish stripes, is worth planting behind the black leaves of *Colocasia*, or against *Solenostemon* 'Lemon Dash', or, as in my garden, under *Clematis viticella* 'Alba Luxurians', or under *Hakonechloa macra* 'Aureola', a Japanese grass, with green-striped, yellow leaves. All of these make balanced colour combinations.

A border of softer colours, with different shades of purple through to pink, can be equally stunning. Whites are brilliant too. The large *Crambe cordifolia* has a massive, creamy-white, gypsophylla-like, faintly scented flowerhead. Also try the elegant *Zantedeschia aethiopica*, with its white spathe, or, for slightly more colour, the very attractive *Z. a.* 'Green Goddess', with a cream spathe edged with green. Alternatively, you can mix the more muted colours with intense, bright colours. What you grow should depend on where your own particular colour fantasy takes you.

Salvias are wonderful for adding blues and purples to the border, as well as red, and should be used more widely, especially as their flowering season lasts until the first frosts. The flowers of *Salvia patens* 'Cambridge Blue', carried on tall stems, are the richest of blues. *S.* 'Indigo Spires', a hybrid between *S. farinacea* and *S. longispicata*, carries long spikes of deep indigo-blue flowers late into the autumn. It looks striking when planted behind *Melianthus major*, which has grey-green to blue-green leaflets. *S. discolor* is a personal favourite. The leaves are green on top and densely woolly white beneath, less hairy above. Racemes of indigo-black flowers catch the waning autumn sun. I keep a large pot of this salvia near my front door for its late flowers, and for its perfume when the leaves are crushed.

PREVIOUS PAGES *This border of succulents can be seen at Tresco Abbey in the Isles of Scilly. The garden experiences fairly cold winters, yet it is able to support a number of exotic-looking plants, including aeoniums, Lampranthus varieties, and an aloe.*

LEFT *Redolent of the tropics, this hot border is actually located in the temperate zone of the northern hemisphere. Plants that contribute to the luxuriant setting include the annual spider flower Cleome hassleriana 'Colour Fountain' (left foreground), the vibrant Lobelia species (to its right), and the equally stunning Plectranthus argentatus (far right). A clump of purple-leaved canna and the bamboo-like grass Arundo donax 'Variegata' complete the picture.*

RIGHT *Plants with violet flowers, such as this Lobelia species, add vibrancy to the exotic garden, where a colour scheme can be planned around cool, as well as hot, colours.*

Agapanthus are a must for the more Mediterranean-style garden. Coming from South Africa, they are accustomed to strong sun and hot summer conditions. They come in shades that range from dark blue to white.

Alliums are bulbous perennials whose leaves have usually withered by the time the flowers appear. *Allium cristophii* makes a dramatic impact, with large flowerheads up to 20cm (8in) across and up to 50 pink-purple, star-shaped flowers. Many alliums keep their seedheads after flowering, which gives them interesting architectural shapes. If you grow them between hostas you do not have to see the allium leaves dying down in late spring. The individual flowers of *A. schubertii* are carried on both long and short stalks. *A. hollandicum* 'Purple Sensation' has deep violet flowerheads 5–7cm (2–3in) across: an exciting plant for early summer. Clematis also provide good colour, especially the large-flowering varieties. The species *C. heracleifolia* is self-supporting and has blue-purple flowers in late summer. *Tweedia caerulea* grows well in pots and is a more intense powdery blue than *C. heracleifolia*. The pale-blue flowers look stunning sprawling through the stronger blue of the grass *Elymus magellanicus*.

The bright orange of Crocosmia masoniorum *overhangs a* Solenostemon *species. The young banana* Ensete ventricosum *provides a broad backdrop of verdant green, while in the top left corner are the vibrant orange flowers of a Mexican sunflower,* Tithonia rotundifolia.

Close planting of Clivia miniata *at the Orto Botanico, Palermo, Sicily. In areas prone to frosts, these voluptuous plants can only be grown outside in containers during the summer, as they resent root disturbance and need a restricted root run to flower well.*

Cobaea scandens, the cup and saucer plant, is a perennial that grows as easily as a fast-growing annual. The flowers start off yellowy-green, but become rich purple as they mature. Grown from seed, the plant will cover the whole side of a house by the autumn. For first-time growers of exotica, this is a good, easy plant. Others are the annual *Ipomoea tricolor* 'Heavenly Blue', the morning glory, and the perennial *I. indica*, which has rich purple-blue flowers, and evergreen heart-shaped leaves.

The purple-red flowers of *Knautia macedonica* contrast well with dark-leaved, purple dahlias or purple cordyline. This plant is quite hardy, and although it does not have an exotic appearance it is useful for the colourful contribution it makes to the garden throughout the summer.

One of the most colourful foliage plants to grow – if you are bold enough and can accommodate it – is the Abyssinian or Ethiopian banana *Ensete ventricosum* 'Maurelii'. Nothing compares with it for sheer size, the intensity of the deep maroon-purple leaves, and its speed of growth. If you keep it through the winter, it goes from a 60cm (24in) plant to one that reaches 5m (15ft) in three years. I underplant this purple monster with the green leaves of *Alocasia macrorrhiza*, which has ribbed, mid-green foliage. Although the leaves reach 60cm (2ft), they still look small compared with the banana – rather like David and Goliath in form. The effect of light on the purple banana is very dramatic; when the sun shines through the leaves, the colours change, creating a stunning effect.

RIGHT *The iridescent* Caladium bicolor *'Red Flash' makes an excellent plant for bedding out during the summer. It is tropical in origin, so, if the summers are unpredictable, it is advisable to grow it in a pot and bring it in if the weather suddenly turns cold.*

LEFT *The flowers of the cup and saucer plant,* Cobaea scandens, *will sometimes last well into the autumn. Grown from seed sown in spring, this climber will grow as much as 9.1m (30ft) in one season. In frost-free climates it is perennial and will grow to as much as 20m (70ft).*

RIGHT **Solenostemon** *(syn.* **Coleus***) was widely used by the Victorians for massed bedding. Also known as the flame nettle, or painted nettle, this is a family of easily propagated plants whose striking leaves are available in virtually every colour combination, with the exception of blue.*

During the day, colours in the garden tend to be rather flat, but as evening arrives many plant colours become more pronounced. Many white flowering plants, such as *Zantedeschia aethiopica* 'Crowborough', which has a creamy-white spathe, simply glow at twilight. Effective orange colours include *Tithonia rotundifolia* 'Torch', and *Hemerocallis* 'Burning Daylight', the latter a pulsating, yellow-orange.

When planting with colour in mind, try to avoid a 'pincushion' effect, where you get bright colours dotted against more muted ones. Rather, keep clumps of bright colours together – for example, *Canna* 'Striata' with red *Lobelia cardinalis*, where the intense red of the lobelia flower on its dark-purple foliage stands out against the green and yellow stripes of the canna – a truly stunning combination.

The canna family has varieties with green, dark-purple, or almost black leaves, topped with racemes of intensely coloured flowers: the hybrids *C.* 'Australia' and *C.* 'Durban' (*C.* 'Tropicanna' in the U.S.A.) are good examples. All cannas have large, showy flowers in gorgeous shades.

If you prefer not to live permanently with hot colours, you might like to grow annuals. Nasturtiums, such as the red-flowering *Tropaeolum majus* 'Empress of India', and the double ones, such as the orange *T. m.* 'Hermine Grashoff' and yellow *T. m.* 'Darjeeling Gold', are terrific for colour.

A view across a section of planting at Beth Chatto's extensive gravel garden in Essex, England, showing the more muted colours of a border that is not irrigated at all during the summer, so that the plants have to be tough and fend for themselves. At the top is a large specimen of Euphorbia characias *subsp.* wulfenii. *Below that are varieties of oriental poppy with, in the centre, an eryngium species, and, on the left, catmint (*Nepeta*).*

Cleome hassleriana *'Colour Fountain' (foreground) has dainty flowers and strangely scented leaves. Here it is planted with a dark-purple-leaved, red-flowering canna and, to the right, the clump-forming* Lobelia x gerardii *'Vedrariensis'.*

The vigorous early flowering Clematis armandii *is the only evergreen species of clematis that grows successfully outdoors in the northern hemisphere. It is also notable for the exceptionally fragrant perfume produced by its large white flowers.*

For the glorious colour of their foliage, try such plants as *Maranta* and *Aglaonema*, or, one of my favourites, *Solenostemon*. This plant really does seem to prefer being outside in summer, where it will reach 90cm (36in) rather than the 30cm (12in) it reaches inside. These are architectural plants that come in colours from yellow to purple. S. 'Black Prince' is a dark purple-black – the complete opposite to S. 'Lemon Dash'. Grown together they look ridiculously bright. S. 'Winter Sun' is a vivid orange. Again, don't think of them as houseplants, just think of them as plants.

Begonias are also excellent for brightening darker corners, especially some of the larger-flowered, tuberous varieties. I find that many of those usually grown as houseplants are particularly appealing when planted en masse, and they also make unusual and exotic ground cover when in dappled moist shade. Bromeliads and similar species also make excellent summer bedding, or they can be wired to the side of *Dicksonia antarctica* (see p.96). *Tillandsia cyanea* has flat, almost stalkless, rose-pink spikes, and unusual purple flowers pop out of the top.

Many shrubs make colourful and hardy backdrops in the garden. One of the best for purple is the smoke bush, *Cotinus coggygria* 'Royal Purple', which has rich purple-pink leaves and fuzzy purple flowers in the summer. However, I don't let mine flower as I only want the colourful foliage. *Cotinus* looks particularly good against the grass *Arundo donax* 'Variegata'. The yellow shrub *Sambucus racemosa* 'Plumosa Aurea', and the black *S. nigra* are equally nice and will grow up to 2m (6 ft) if pollarded annually.

RIGHT *Agapanthus (seen here in close-up) are very exotic-looking plants from South Africa. The evergreen species occur mainly in coastal areas, while the deciduous species tend to grow in more alpine regions of grassland.*

BELOW *The somewhat grass-like leaves of the amazingly black Ophiopogon planiscapus 'Nigrescens' bear a startling resemblence to shredded plastic. This is a spreading plant with short, bell-shaped, pinkish-white flowers carried on short stems.*

RIGHT *Agapanthus, lobelia (in the foreground), and varieties of purple-leaved cannas combine to provide a palette of soft tones. They are grown here with the striped green-and-yellow zebra grass, Miscanthus sinensis 'Zebrinus' (centre top).*

If you take the risk, you can have a really colourful border by using such plants as abutilons. They are fairly tender but extremely exotic looking, especially some of the very 'ritzy' variegated forms such as *Abutilon pictum* 'Thompsonii', which has green leaves that are mottled with yellow. The delicate nodding flowers are orange flushed with salmon pink.

Dig the plants up in the autumn and keep them frost free, then replant in spring. There are a few species that are frost hardy: *A. vitifolium* is fast growing, with purplish-blue flowers in late spring/early summer, reaching a height of 4m (12ft). The variety 'Album' looks tropical, but isn't; its flowers are pure white. *A. x suntense* is a large plant suitable for the back of a warm, sunny border, while the variety *A. s.* 'Violetta' has dark violet flowers that are 7cm (3in) across.

The more tender hybrid *A.* 'Ashford Red' has nodding, pendent red flowers, and *A.* 'Boule de Neige' white flowers. Both can be grown in pots or in the ground, but they must be brought inside in the autumn unless you live in a warm favourable climate with little or no frost.

Dahlias are now back in fashion – not grown, as traditionally, in rows, but interplanted with other plants. There are quite a few with purple leaves, such as *D.* 'Bishop of Llandaff', a beautiful old cultivar with intense red flowers and blackish-red foliage. *D.* 'Bednall Beauty', similar in colour, is more compact and doesn't need staking, while *D.* 'Moonfire' produces single, apricot-yellow flowers with a red tint. Some of the larger-flowered varieties with green leaves are also worth considering, such as *D.* 'Zorro', with scarlet flowers, or the smaller *D.* 'Jescot Julie', an orchid-flowered variety.

the lush, jungle-style garden

The cool and lush exotic garden is evocative of thick forest or woodland in warm and subtropical climates. It creates the sensation of peace, a world away from the hubbub of everyday life. Moisture, shade, and abundant plantings are the requirements of this style of garden. Foliage is absolutely essential, particularly in the different shades of luxuriant green that the plant kingdom has to offer.

Spiky plants can make dramatic statements when placed among rounded, broad-leaved, or even feathery ones. One of the best in this category is the clump-forming perennial *Phormium tenax*, with its majestic, smooth, grey-green leaves – a truly dramatic plant that produces a rapier-like effect as its leaves carve through the air. This is the hardiest phormium species, and probably the toughest. In summer, stout, red-purple flower panicles thrust above the foliage to 4m (12ft) – as dramatic a flower as the plant that produced it. *P. cookianum* has broad, linear leaves. They arch over in a flowing fashion, and grow to a length of 1.5m (5ft), so they are better for the smaller garden.

If you want an even smaller plant, *P .t.* 'Dazzler', only 90cm (36in) high, is a very accommodating species, with arching, bronze leaves that have red, orange, and pink tips. However, the more colourful phormiums tend to be the least hardy, so in temperate regions I would only plant the very exotic ones in a sheltered, urban garden, or in the warmer areas of the south. *P. tenax* can, however, be grown quite successfully outdoors.

RIGHT *This tranquil, exotic, urban garden includes a pollarded* Paulownia tomentosa *(top left), a* Trachycarpus *variety (top centre at the back), and ginger varieties (centre). The garden demonstrates how much can easily be accomplished in a small, confined area – probably only a short distance away from other gardens, but nevertheless providing a sense of tranquillity removed from the hustle and bustle of city life.*

BELOW *A stately multi-branching* Aeonium arboreum *makes a dramatic contrast to the large leaves of the European or dwarf fan palm,* Chamaerops humilis.

Another species that bristles with waving spikes is *Cordyline australis*. Even when young it is a very thrusting plant that forms a dome of strap-like leaves. The cordylines can be grown in containers and brought inside for the winter. This is especially advisable for the variegated varieties such as *C. a.* 'Albertii'. As with the phormiums, the more colourful they are, the more tender. However, the hardier species, such as *C. australis,* may survive the winter outside if given protection when young (*see p. 92*).

Grasses and reeds are excellent spiky plants too. The huge *Miscanthus sacchariflorus* easily reaches 3m (10ft) in one season. If the summer growth is left through the winter, the leaves gradually turn brown. *Arundo donax* is another tall plant for the cool, lush garden that grows to a similar height as the miscanthus. It has wide, grey, floating foliage, with leaves that are carried alternately on both sides of stiff vertical stems. *A. d.* 'Variegata' is a green-and-cream version which looks stunning planted against dark-leaved cannas or colocasias. However, it is not as hardy as the species.

LEFT *A jungle setting in Myles Challis's garden in London shows how tightly packed a small plot can be. The plants include some young, purple bananas, Ensete ventricosum 'Maurelii', as well as a green version. The spiky plants are Cordyline australis.*

RIGHT *This small London garden has an artificial pool that extends to the walls on either side of it, thereby creating the illusion that the garden is much larger than it really is. The vertical culms of the black bamboo* Phyllostachys nigra, *a tall* Cordyline australis, *tree ferns, and palm trees form a thick and lush planting.*

LEFT *The glossy leaves of* Farfugium japonicum *'Aureomaculatum', from Japan, are spotted yellow, as though someone had spilt paint on the leaves. This unusual plant will take a few degrees of frost quite happily, but in colder areas it is best to dig it up and store it in a glasshouse for the winter.*

PREVIOUS PAGES *In the garden at La Mortola (Giardini Botanici Hanbury), near Ventimiglia, Italy, stone steps curve around the back of a pool, above which is* Cyperus papyrus. *Large aloes guard the tops of the stairways. At the back of the pool are the large, thrusting leaves of a water canna, planted next to a* Colocasia *species. Both plants can be grown either directly in water or in moist ground.*

LEFT *A small suburban town garden planted with palms and bamboos, the evergreen pittosporum, and a ginger,* Hedychium gardnerianum *(centre). The exotic, evergreen* Thalia dealbata, *grown for its long-stalked, lance-shaped leaves, and attractive violet flowers, is growing in the pool.*

ABOVE RIGHT *Leaves of the bamboo* Sasa palmata *are shown here in close-up, illustrating the intriguing effects that sunlight makes as it passes through the foliage.*

ABOVE FAR RIGHT *The bamboo* Phyllostachys dulsi *produces particularly attractive culms, up to 8cm (3in) in diameter. The shoots of this 5m- (15-ft) tall, clump-forming bamboo can be eaten when the plant is young.*

Bamboos are a must for the cool, lush garden, and many of the taller ones, such as *Phylostachys bambusoides*, and *P. nigra*, can be used for screening. Dwarf bamboos include *Sasa veitchii at* 1.2m (4ft) tall, with leaves up to 6cm (2⅖in) wide and 25cm (10in) long. It can be a bit of a thug in the garden, so needs containing by a low wall or tiles sunk into the ground. During the winter the leaves tend to wither, creating light-buff-coloured margins that look very attractive. *S. palmata* has similar foliage, but at 2.5m (8ft) plus is taller. It is also invasive and best contained, but is well worth growing for the leafy, jungle-like effect it creates as it hangs over a path.

Bamboos are filamentous and upright. A complete contrast to these and other tall species are large-leaved plants such as the aroids. *Alocasia macrorrhiza* can be bedded out for the summer months, or kept in a large pot. The large leaves are glossy, arrow-shaped, and heavily veined. In temperate climes they will reach a length of 60–90cm (2–3ft) on equally long stems, but they grow even larger when planted in water, or in warmer regions. This stunning plant is a close relative of *Colocasia esculenta*, one of most exotic plants you can grow outside in temperate zones. The massive leaves, measuring 90cm x 60cm (3ft x 2ft), are heart shaped.

LEFT *The soft, feathery leaves of* Adiantum venustum *mingle with the fronds of the larger-leaved* Polypodium. *Ferns are very useful for creating a cool, lush effect in dappled shade under trees. They were very popular with the Victorians, who used to create special areas for them, called ferneries, in their gardens.*

RIGHT *The two large, pineapple-like flowerheads belong to* Eucomis bicolor, *planted on either side of a* Solenostemon *cultivar. Other species shown include the banana* Ensete ventricosum *'Red Stripe' and (left) the dahlia D. 'Yellow Hammer'.*

No lush garden can exist without ferns, one of the most popular being the tree fern. In its natural habitat the air is very moist, so cultivated species must be grown in damp areas, or where there is an irrigation system that allows water to drip into them. Shade or semi-shade is another essential requirement, as sun burns the foliage. The better you treat these plants, and the more moisture you give them, the more they will thrive.

The fronds grow quickly from a new shoot to a mature frond in a few weeks. Ideally, they would be planted in a grove, with trees at various stages of development, and at staggered heights – for example, one 2.5m (8ft) tall, one 1.5m (5ft), one 60cm (24in), and so on. Underplant with the ordinary, tough, male fern, *Dryopteris filix-mas*, or the hard shield fern, *Polysticum aculeatum*. For very lush underplanting, and soft, feathery foliage, try the maidenhair fern *Adiantum pedatum* or *A. venustum*. Any one of the many *Adiantum* forms will look gorgeous when grown outside.

It is possible to plant into the trunk of the tree fern. I have done so with the common staghorn fern, *Platycerium bifurcatum*. Prise open a small pocket between some of the old frond stems and push some of the roots into the gap. Tie in with wire and keep well watered. Various forms of the bromeliad-like *Tillandsia cyanea* can also be planted in the same way.

ABOVE *The leaves of* Hosta *'Sum and Substance' gradually turn olive-yellow as summer wears on. Hostas are invaluable in the lush, jungle-style garden. There is such a large variety of sizes and leaf colours, and they have a very exotic appearance.*

LEFT *Two newly-fronded tree ferns,* Dicksonia antarctica, *grow happily in a sea of bright orange crocosmias. This garden, at Trebah in Cornwall, England, has groves of these great tree ferns.*

To my mind, bananas are the ultimate in exotica. They are fast-growing, towering, vast herbs that are easy to cultivate. Among the hardiest, *Musa basjoo* is excellent for the lush garden, although the leaves will be torn in high winds, so it is best planted in an area of the garden protected from the prevailing wind. *Ensete ventricosum*, although not hardy, is one to grow for sheer audacity, especially *E. v.* 'Maurelii', which has huge, purple, paddle-like leaves – up to 6m (20ft) long and 60cm (2ft) wide – that thrust skywards from a stout 30cm (12in) wide trunk. It reaches a height of 5m (15ft). This species can be effectively underplanted with alocasias, which, although they are relatively large plants themselves, are almost dwarfed by the size of the banana.

The variety *Ensete ventricosum* 'Red Stripe' contributes an intriguing verticality to the garden. If this variety is too big, there is a far more diminutive banana called *Musa lasiocarpa*, about 1.2m (4ft) tall or more, which has very thick, grey to blue-green leaves. Given good conditions, it will produces myriads of flowers in gorgeous shades of ochre. This attractive species is reputed to be even hardier than *M. basjoo*.

The ginger family is a very exuberant group of plants that are excellent for the lush garden, in both flower and leaf. *Hedychium gardnerianum* is one of the tallest; it often reaches 2.2m (7ft) when in flower. The flowers themselves – bright yellow, with red stamens – are a good 25–35cm (10–14in) long on top of the luscious foliage. They appear from late summer onwards, and emit the most delicious scent. Imagine walking around a corner on a summer evening and finding a clump of these gingers beneath a banana plant. In temperate climates, the impact is such that one is immediately transported to the tropics.

H. coccineum 'Tara' is a hardier variety, but no less exotic. The flowers are orange with red stamens. If you are bit worried about frosts, this is one to grow; it is much less demanding than *H. gardnerianum*, and is fairly hardy when grown outside, especially if covered with straw during the winter months. *H. densiflorum* is one of easiest to grow. It has small, orange flower spikes 15cm (6in) long and 2.5cm (1in) wide. The flowers give off a honey-like scent, but when the stems are snapped they emit a smell like that of camphor. All of these scents are equated with lushness. You will soon notice that in rain almost all the foliage in a lush garden emits a fragrance, in addition to the visual sensations it offers.

ABOVE **Cordyline terminalis,** *normally thought of as a houseplant in cooler climes, actually loves being outside during the summer, where it adds to the jungle effect.* **Helichrysum petiolare** *'Limelight' will easily take a few degrees of frost, but if you do lose a plant it will be very easy to replace, as they grow quickly from cuttings.*

RIGHT *The fiery juvenile foliage of* **Pieris formosa** *var.* forrestii *appears in the spring, followed by panicles of creamy-white, highly scented flowers. It is seen here with the cardoon,* **Cynara cardunculus,** *which towers to a height of 2m (6ft), with purple flowerheads, produced from early to midsummer, that are much loved by bees.*

Brugmansia, angel's trumpet, makes a great contribution to the exotic, lush garden. While the leaves are in various shades of green, the huge flowers are pale pink, yellow, or white. The white flowers of *B. x candida* 'Double White' in particular stand out, giving a distinctly lush feeling, and a sense of coolness. In the evening, their intoxicating scent is overpowering.

On the whole, brugmansias are not particularly hardy, although *B. sanguinea*, with yellow and red trumpets, is said to be root hardy. With most varieties I cut down the stems to 1.5m (5ft) and cut off most of the roots, then put what is left in a black bin liner or a large pot. The plants are replanted in spring when the danger of frost is over. The leaves soon reappear as the plants get their roots down. The size you cut your plants down to in autumn depends on how much room you have to store them; the taller you keep them, the bigger they become the following year.

The cool, lush garden requires the right conditions, and a good deal of work. Whether it is worthwhile depends on how much time you want to put into the garden in order to create something very special. Having done the work, you will find your efforts are well rewarded as you walk around your garden on a sultry evening in high summer.

The hot, dry, Mediterranean-style garden is a more specialized version of the exotic garden; its creators try to evoke those parts of the world that have dry climates with long, hot, summer days, and warm evenings. Although deciduous plants can play an important role here, the overall effect relies on a preponderance of evergreen species that take you through the winter. The planting scheme should be open and airy – after all, these plants grow in open gardens, not enclosed jungles.

The Mediterranean type of climate is also found in other regions of the world, including stretches of California, South Africa, Chile, Australia, and New Zealand. Therefore, no Mediterranean-style garden would be complete without substantial representation from these parts of the world, using perhaps such plants as *Ceanothus* or *Fremontodendron* species from California, many of the spiky-leaved plants from New Zealand, or low-growing, silver, or grey, foliage plants from southern Europe.

However, not every garden in temperate regions can turn on the sunshine in summer to emulate precisely the conditions such plants require, so in many cases gardeners have to try to achieve the Mediterranean feeling by adapting their methods of planting, or by growing species that are similar to those from hotter climates, yet are also tolerant of cooler conditions.

LEFT *Pots and containers cover the author's garden. The filamentous plant on the left is* Verbena bonariensis, *growing in front of* Agave americana. *The container on the table holds the white-flowering Peruvian lily,* Hymenocallis narcissiflora; Cordyline australis *'Albertii' is just beneath it, on the ground.*

BELOW *Gravel helps to provide the well-drained conditions that drought-loving plants require. Here the planting includes the poppy* Papaver orientale *'Juliane' (top left),* Anthemis punctata *subsp.* cupaniana *(left and right), together with a young* Agave americana *'Marginata' (centre). All of these plants grow happily during the summer months without irrigation.*

Plants that thrive in hot, dry climates are able to tolerate a shortage of water and high rates of evaporation. The problem they face in most temperate regions is that there is too much rain, so if they are to survive they must be planted in well-drained, sandy, or gravelly, soil, or grown in raised beds. In clay or heavy loam, the soil must be made lighter by digging in lots of sharp sand, grit, or fine shingle.

Two plants that are very much associated with the Mediterranean are *Bougainvillea* and *Plumbago capensis*. Unfortunately, in a temperate climate they must be grown in containers against warm, south-facing walls or in conservatories. If you want something of similar habit to plant out, you might try growing a clematis such as *Clematis* x *fargesioides* 'Paul Farges' (syn. *C.* 'Summer Snow'). This vigorous species has small, white, star-shaped flowers in late summer, and a great liana-like appearance. Another recommended later-flowering clematis is *C. Jackmanii*, an abundant climber that bears single, velvety, dark-purple flowers with light, green-brown anthers. It grows to a height of at least 3m (10ft), and creates a bougainvillea-like effect. *Campsis radicans* is probably one of the most exotic-looking flowering climbers that can be grown outside in temperate climes. It has deep, orange-red, trumpet-shaped blossoms, and flowers from late summer through to the autumn.

LEFT *This Mediterranean-style border in the author's garden contains plants from around the world. The New Zealand flax,* Phormium tenax, *towers above the spiky flowers of* Acanthus spinosus. *The aromatic leaves of a bergamot add fragrance, while cool tones are represented by a purple lobelia, and blue* Agapanthus Headbourne hybrids. *Below these, hotter colours are provided by the annual* Cosmos sulphureus, *and the young, green flower-clusters of* Sedum 'Herbstfreude' (syn. 'Autumn Joy') *will become a deep wine red in the autumn.*

RIGHT *Pots and containers are almost essential in a Mediterranean-style garden. They can be used to brighten up a corner of the garden or courtyard. The centrepiece here is an* Agave americana 'Marginata', *with, beneath it, a variety of blue-grey* Echeveria. *The pink flowers are those of an ivy-leaved pelargonium.*

ABOVE *The budding flowerheads and the leaf-stalks of the globe artichoke,* Cynara scolymus. *If blanched, the leaf-stalks can be eaten as a vegetable. However, if you can refrain from eating the plant, the thistle-like flowers are well worth waiting for.*

Many of the alliums are wonderful plants to grow in the garden. They are very much Mediterranean plants, growing in the wild in sparse, grassy areas, where they come into full growth and flower early in the season. By the time the heat of high summer arrives, both the flowers and the leaves have died away, although the seedheads remain. The seedhead of *Allium* 'Globemaster' has a head up to 15cm (6in) across; that of *A.* 'Purple Sensation' is 8cm (3in) across. Plants from the Californian chaparral, which corresponds closely to the Mediterranean in climate, include Californian fuchsias, *Zauschneria* species, quite low-growing, gorgeous plants, with fiery, orangey-red flowers from summer to autumn. The tree poppy, *Romneya coulteri*, is another Californian species. A tall plant, growing up to 2.5m (8ft) high, it has silvery-grey foliage, and huge white flowers.

Eryngiums are fantastic plants for growing in the hot, dry garden. Species are found all over the world, often on mountain slopes. They thrive in full sun and well-drained soil, whether it is alkaline, sandy, or gravely. *E. giganteum*, known as Miss Willmott's ghost, is a perennial reaching up to 90cm (36in), with stout branches, and very silvery cones surrounded by metallic, silver-green bracts. Although it is very free seeding and can be a nuisance, it is undoubtedly one of the loveliest plants for growing in the dry garden.

ABOVE *Large agapanthus specimens stand on either side of the door to a potting shed at the Od Vicarage, East Ruston, Norfolk, England. The walls of the shed are covered with the variegated* Trachelospermum jasminoides. *Below the window a mixture of succulents is displayed on wooden shelves. To the right can be seen a few fronds of the blue-grey, evergreen shrub* Melianthus major.

RIGHT *This gravel bed at Beth Chatto's garden in Essex, England, contains a group of small, grey-leaved* Senecio *species, and a sprawling clump of the dark-leaved* Sedum telephium *subsp.* maximum *'Atropurpureum'. Below this is a daintily stalked* Tulbaghia violacea.

Native to Europe and North Africa, rock roses, *Cistus* species, are obviously well adapted to drought. They are inclined to be tender in colder districts with heavy soil, but are tougher on poor, sandy soil. Although the individual white, or dark-pink, flowers last only a day, they are produced in abundance and with a butterfly-like charm from early to late summer.

Cistus are also enjoyed for their warm-green to grey-green leaves, some of which have intensely strong, oily scents. One of the best for felted foliage is *C. albidus*, which has very pale, almost white, foliage in hot summers, and pale lilac flowers. Unfortunately, it is one of the least hardy and needs a very sheltered position, although it is still well worth growing for its Mediterranean effect. *C. x corbariensis* is hardier, making a compact bush, eventually 1m (3ft) or so tall and round. It has closely crinkled foliage, with attractive brown tints in late winter. The flowers have very conspicuous, red buds opening to small, white cups with yellow centres. *C. 'Silver Pink'* is another excellent form that seems to be quite tough. It has narrow, dark-green leaves, and deep-pink flowers with pale centres.

Artemisias are found in wasteland and rocky areas in the northern hemisphere. They are a large family, mainly of aromatic perennials with wonderful feathery foliage, and are well adapted to drought conditions. Two of the best are *Artemisia absinthium* 'Lambrook Silver', which has silvery-grey leaves, and *A.* 'Powis Castle', which has billowing,, feathery silver-grey leaflets. Both these artemisias should be cut back hard in spring to renew bushy growth.

ABOVE *Drops of moisture remain on the rosettes of* Aeonium 'Zwartkop' *after rain. Its stunning, black-purple leaves make this a popular succulent for summer bedding.*

RIGHT *The highly scented* Lilium regale *is planted near the entrance to the author's house. A collection of succulents and cacti, including an aeonium, crassulas, agaves, and aloes, grows in containers on the steps, and a European or dwarf fan palm,* Chamaerops humilis, *stands behind the posts.*

PREVIOUS PAGES *This dry, gravel garden contains a mixed planting of Mediterranean-style plants. In the middle, a swathe of* Stipa tenacissima *is surrounded by* Eryngium giganteum, Verbena, *and* Anthemis. *Top left are the drying seedheads of alliums, while in the centre background are* Verbascum *and swathes of* Crambe cordifolia.

LEFT *A path meanders through a Mediterranean planting, which includes the spiky leaves of New Zealand flax,* Phormium tenax, *and, in the foreground, an* Eryngium *species.*

RIGHT *An intriguing collection of tall* Cerus *cacti species and bromeliads grows in the shade of a tree, illustrating how spectacular effects can be created in a Mediterranean-style garden by using just one or two families of plant. Lotusland at Montecito, California, is definitely a hot, dry, fantasy garden.*

Of the cacti, one of my favourites is *Agave americana*, which is native to North America, from Mexico into southern Arizona. In the wild it can be enormous, up to 2–3m (6–10ft) high. This agave is grown in parts of the Mediterranean, in Spain and Greece, where the massive flower spikes reach a height of 6–8m (20–25ft). In temperate climes it will not reach that height. *A. a.* 'Marginata', which is green with a yellow edge, will grow up to about 30–60cm (24–36in) high and round in a container. It can also be grown outside in the ground, in a dry bed, and can be left outside all winter if protected with a sheet of glass or plastic. In warmer temperate areas it may actually grow to as much as 1.2m (4ft). Many of the succulents and cacti can be grown outside if they are kept dry. In northern Arizona I have seen agaves and opuntias growing in temperatures as low as −10 to −15°C (5–14°F). However, it is a very dry cold; agaves don't like winters that are cold and damp. If water gets into the crowns and freezes, the plant will become mushy and die. This applies to most of the plants mentioned here: if you grow them dry, or as dry as you can, that is, in well-drained soil, they will take much colder temperatures.

Opuntias are very much associated with hot, dry places. In the Mediterranean region they are found growing in Spain, Greece, Israel, Tunisia, and Morocco. But although associated with Old World countries, opuntias are in fact native to North, Central, and South America. Most have pad-shaped leaves that are sometimes cylindrical but usually flat. Treat them with care as they can be exceedingly vicious.

Among the spiky cacti, the yuccas – which also come from the Americas – have great dominance and form in the garden. They are spectacular when used as architectural specimens in patios, courtyards, or borders. One of my favourites is *Yucca whipplei*, a clump-forming, stemless plant with interesting linear, finely-toothed, rigid, grey-green leaves up to 90cm (36in) long. If you are lucky enough to get the yucca to flower, it will produce a huge flower spike of spectacular, creamy panicles on a stem up to 2m (6ft) tall or more. *Y. gloriosa* is one of the most common yucca species. It has stiffly pointing, arching leaves, up to 60cm (24in) long, which become blue-green as they mature – in the right setting the plant gives a truly desert-like feeling. There is another version, *Y. g.* 'Variegata', which has yellow-margined leaves. This is an especially valuable plant for the garden because its colouring creates a summery effect even in winter.

LEFT *Bright red inner leaves surround the tightly packed flowers of the bromeliad* Fascicularia pitcairniifolia. *This plant has survived in the author's garden for over a decade, with only slight frost damage during the winter months, and despite attacks by woodlice, which seem to enjoy eating the flowers.*

BELOW *The large agave at the Jardin Exotique de Roscoff, Brittany, France, is surrounded by pelargoniums, anthemis, and lampranthus. In the distance is a flowering* Cordyline australis, *and, to the left of it, the purple-blue flower stems of* Echium.

a practical guide to exotic gardening

Cultivating exotic plants

This section covers various aspects of exotic plant care, including the general care of cordylines, cannas, gingers, and tree ferns, and the planting out of cacti and succulents. It also considers the general maintenance of bamboos, especially the more invasive types, as well as the various methods of propagating *Solenostemon* (*Coleus*) and aeoniums. There are obviously many more plants than are mentioned here that have similar care or propagation requirements. The rule with the more tender exotic plants (houseplants) is to be aware of the lowest temperatures that occur in their natural habitats. Although many exotic plants (other than hothouse varieties) grow well outside during the warmer months in temperate climates, most should come into a glasshouse or conservatory when the temperature drops below 7–10°C (44–50°F).

Cordyline australis

As *Cordyline australis* can take several degrees of frost quite happily, it grows well in temperate regions. However, it is advisable to protect young plants until they have become established. With time, these plants form multi-headed trees of some stature. They grow more quickly in deep soil, as they then produce a large, carrot-like root. Cordylines can be grown as specimens in a flower and shrub border, or in a courtyard. They also look good when planted in a group of plants of varying sizes. They will grow in large containers for some years, although those grown like this will never become as large as those planted in the ground. Try to protect them from high winds. These plants are now easy to find in nurseries and fairly inexpensive. Of the many new varieties on the market, the more colourful ones tend to be less hardy.

PLANTING OUT CORDYLINES

It is best to plant them out when they have at least 15cm (6in) of trunk (older plants are hardier than younger ones). Ease the plant out of the container and carefully tease out the roots. Plant in deep, humus-rich, well-drained soil.

WINTER CARE OF CORDYLINES

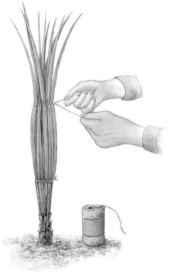

1 To protect from frost when young, wrap the leaves with raffia, or string, to protect the crown. Very young plants should be kept frost free until large enough to be planted out.

2 In colder climates, wrap the plant with several layers of horticultural fleece or sacking. Place some dry straw around the base, keepng it in place with wire mesh or bricks.

Cacti

In temperate climates, most cacti and succulents grow well outside in pots and containers during the warmer months of the year. They can also be bedded out in a south-facing aspect once the danger of frost has passed. Cacti prefer a bed of very well-drained, gritty soil. Some of the tallest, such as *Cerus* species, might need staking to prevent them from falling over. Succulents and cacti such as agaves and opuntias will take quite severe frost if they can be kept dry. However, if you want to keep these plants outside in wetter areas it is advisable to cover them with waterproof protection.

PLANTING OUT CACTI

1 After the last frost, arrange the cacti and succulents into their planting positions, trying to make them look irregular and natural.

2 When planting, make sure that the soil is well drained and gritty, as otherwise these desert plants will rot. Always use gloves when handling.

3 Place small gravel, grit, or rock chippings around the plants for a more natural effect; this also aids drainage, and stops their bases rotting.

Cannas

Cannas are readily obtained in most garden centres in late winter or early spring. Most of them come in plastic bags, so check the tubers by feeling them to see if they are firm, have not dried out, or are not rotten. Suppliers of cannas can also be found on the Internet: there are now many nurseries around the world selling plants online. Cannas are easy to grow and propagate, and they bulk up readily over the years, provided that they are planted out in temperate climates after all danger of frost is over. In cool but frost-free areas they can be left in the ground in the autumn, and just covered with straw or a similar material. Otherwise, dig them up after the frost has blackened the leaves, lift them, cut off the foliage, and store in a frost-free place. Check the plants several times during the winter to see if any have rotted; if they have, discard them.

BRINGING CANNAS INTO GROWTH

1 Plant tubers in 15-cm (6-in) pots in general potting compost. Make sure the growing shoots are pointing upwards. Cover the tubers with just enough soil for the shoots to appear above the surface.

2 Place in a propagator, or warm airing cupboard at a minimum of 20°C (69°F). Keep soil moist, but not wet, until shoots appear.

3 Once the shoots have reached 13–20cm (5–8in), they can be moved to cooler conditions, at a min. 10°C (50°F), either in a glasshouse, conservatory, or on a windowsill.

4 After all risk of frost is over, plant in the garden in sun or dappled shade. Add blood, fish, and bone. or a similar fertilizer, to the soil when planting. Mulch with compost or well-rotted manure.

PREPARING CANNAS FOR WINTER

1 After the first frost has blackened the canna's leaves, cut down the foliage to within approx. 5–8cm (2–3in) of the ground.

2 Dig up the plants, being careful not to spike the tubers with the fork. Shake off excess soil, and leave to dry out for a few days in a dry, airy place. Label tubers correctly for each variety.

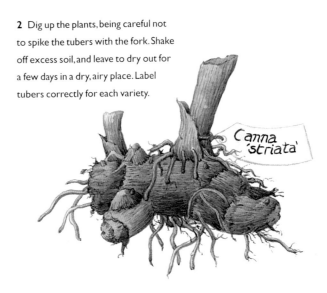

Canna 'striata'

3 Store in old orange boxes or similar containers filled with dry bark chippings or peat. The cannas can be placed in layers if you have a lot of them. Check occasionally during the winter, and discard any rotted tubers.

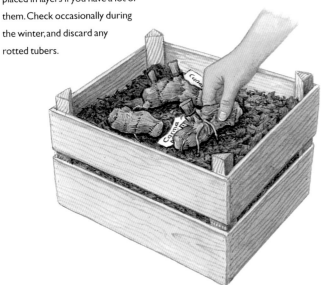

Gingers

Gingers are easy to grow and propagate. Their division and propagation is similar to that of cannas, with some varieties being hardy enough to be left in the ground. When dividing the plants, make sure that there are at least one or two growth buds on each section. Those that are left in the ground should be covered over with a thick mulch of straw during the winter.

DIVIDING GINGERS

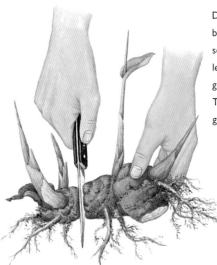

Divide clumps in early spring, by cutting a rhizome into sections with a sharp knife, leaving at least one or two growing points per section. Then replant the sections in groups of three or five.

Tree ferns

As very ancient plants, these large members of the fern family need a certain respect. Placed in the right conditions for growth, large canopies of fronds will be produced every year. However, remember that these moisture-loving plants should have moist trunks at all times – the trunk is, in fact, a root system extended into the air. If you live in an area with dry summers, you will need some sort of misting system, as well as irrigation in the form of water dripping very slowly into the crown. A very thin, straw-like pipe, obtainable from most garden centres, is usually used for this.

1 Plant in a shaded position. Dig a hole slightly larger than the container, and put a small amount of leafmould in the bottom. Plant the fern to the same depth as in the container. If you purchase a non-potted trunk, place approximately 15cm (6in) of the trunk in the ground for stability.

2 Keep the crown and trunk moist at all times. The best way to do this is to pin small-bore irrigation tubing to the side of the trunk, and then bend the nozzle into the crown, where it will slowly drip.

PREPARING TREE FERNS FOR WINTER

The main part of the tree fern that needs protecting against protracted freezing temperatures is the crown. Bend some of the older fronds into the middle before adding extra straw, to protect the growing tip of the plant.

Alocasias and colocasias

Alocasias and colocasias are much tougher than they appear, being able to withstand temperatures down to 0°C (32°F) without much damage to the leaves. The roots can take several degrees of frost if well mulched with straw, or a similar material, during the coldest months of the year.

If you live in a climate where there are frosts over a prolonged period, it is best to dig up the tubers and store them in dry, frost-free conditions during the winter, then restart them in spring. As both alocasias and colocasias are very fast growing, they will soon make substantial plants.

PLANTING ALOCASIAS AND COLOCASIAS

1 Plant tubers in good compost in 15-cm (6-in) or larger pots, depending on the tuber size, with the tops just showing.

2 Place in a warm propagating frame or an airing cupboard, min. 20°C (69°F), until the shoots are 13–15cm (5–6in) high. Then grow on in slightly cooler conditions.

3 After being hardened off, and when all danger of frost is over, the plants can be planted out. They appreciate some good compost or well-rotted manure, both in the hole and as a mulch on top. Plant approx. 30cm (1ft) apart.

WINTER CARE OF ALOCASIAS AND COLOCASIAS

1 If you want the foliage to go through the winter, dig the plants up before the first frost, and grow them on, as houseplants, in a light, warm, airy place. Otherwise, cut the foliage off just above the tuber. If you only experience light frosts in your region, you can cover the tubers in the ground with straw or dry leaves.

2 Dug-up tubers should be placed in a dry, airy place to dry out for a few days before being stored in frost-free conditions. Store them in a similar way to cannas.

Bananas

The hardiest of the bananas, *Musa basjoo*, should be planted out when all danger of frost is over. Put some compost, or well-rotted manure under the plants to help establish good root systems. In autumn, cut the leaves off and place a large drainpipe or chimney-pot over the stem. Fill the gaps with straw, and place a tile on the top. When the clumps are larger, you can use wooden pallets to build a tower around the plants.

Ensete species of banana are not hardy, and must be dug up in the autumn. Fairly small plants can be stored in a frost-free glasshouse or a cool room for the winter. The larger plants require more drastic measures. After the first frost has blackened the leaves, cut them all off, dig up the roots, and remove most of them. Keep the roots dry in a frost-free place until the spring.

HOW TO WRAP FOR WINTER

1 After the first frost has blackened and wilted the leaves, cut them off at the base of the leaf stalk, leaving the upright stem.

2 Nail two wooden pallets, or something similar, together, being careful not to damage the soft stems.

3 Add two more pallets to make a box shape, approx. 1m (3ft) square. Use long nails in order to get through the different layers of wood.

5 If your banana stalks are taller than 1m (3ft), add another layer of pallets on top. When the desired height is reached, top off with roofing felt to protect the plant from rain.

4 Add straw from a bale, puffing it up as you put it in so that it traps more air. You will need approx. two bales per square metre/cubic yard.

ALTERNATIVE METHOD FOR SMALLER BANANAS

1 Cut off the leaves of a single-stemmed banana at their base. Then place a chimney-pot or drainpipe over the top and pack with straw.

2 Cover the top of the pot or pipe with something that won't blow off during winter storms, such as an old roof or flooring tile.

Solenostemon

In more temperate climates, solenostemons are traditionally grown as houseplants, although they make excellent summer bedding plants. They are easy to propagate and very rewarding plants to grow; they also make very fast growth. Keep them bushy and prevent them from going to seed by removing the flowerheads as soon as they appear. These plants will root easily at almost any time of year, although autumn or early spring are the best times. Solenostemons rooted in the autumn tend to make larger plants in the following year, although spring cuttings will soon catch up.

PROPAGATING SOLENOSTEMON BY THE WATER METHOD

1 Take several cuttings, 8–12cm (3–5in) long, from the parent plant. Cut through the stem, just below a leaf node.

2 Carefully remove the first (and on a larger cutting, the second) pair of leaves with a sharp knife.

3 Place several cuttings in a container of water, where they will root in 7–10 days. Living-room temperature is sufficient, if they are placed on a windowsill out of the sun.

4 Pot up rooted cuttings into 8-cm (3-in) pots, and grow on, placing on a windowsill, or in a glasshouse, keeping them at a min. of 15°C (60°F). Shade from bright sun until established.

5 After hardening off, and once all danger of frost is over, plant out approx. 30cm (1ft) apart, feeding with a general fertilizer. Pinch out the growing tip to encourage branching.

PROPAGATING BY THE STANDARD METHOD

Fill a pot with either seed compost, horticultural sand, or perlite. Place cuttings around the edge of the pot, cover it with a polythene bag, and secure with a rubber band. Place on a shady windowsill. Otherwise grow in a propagator, at a min. of 15°C (60°F).

Aeoniums

There are approximately 30 species of this beautiful succulent, a native of the Canary Islands, the Mediterranean, and northern Africa. Aeoniums must be some of the most useful of succulents for decorative effect, whether they are grown in pots or in the ground. They are peerless for their beauty in shape and form when planted in raised beds, either on their own or mixed with other succulents and cacti. However, unlike most cacti, these succulents are not truly drought tolerant, and respond well to being watered in very dry conditions.

TAKING STEM CUTTINGS

1 Take cuttings 5–8cm (2–3in) long, then leave on a windowsill or in a glasshouse for approx. seven days for the cut to heal over.

2 Pot one, or several, cuttings into a pot containing a very gritty-sand mix. Water sparingly until roots have formed.

TAKING LEAF CUTTINGS

The individual leaves can also be planted, approx. 1cm (½ in) deep, in a gritty mix. In a few weeks a small plantlet will appear from the base of the leaf.

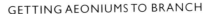

GETTING AEONIUMS TO BRANCH

1 To encourage branching, pinch out the growing tip with your fingernails or a sharp knife. Otherwise, let it grow into a taller plant.

2 Alternatively, with a plant 13–15cm (5–6in) high, cut through the middle. Use the top half as a cutting, and the remaining stump will branch.

Bamboos

Bamboos can be grown in containers at any time of the year. However, the best time to propagate from existing clumps is in the spring and early summer. Divide hardy bamboos in spring, the more tender in late spring or early summer. Try to cut or saw out divisions with at least two or three connected culms (canes). If the divisions are quite large, cut back the top growth by at least 50 percent, so there is less strain on the root system.

Don't expect too much growth in the first year; after that, the bamboo will soon catch up with other plants. The culms of all bamboos have already reached their maximum diameter when they come through the ground in the spring, and usually reach their ultimate size within four to six weeks. If you want them to grow relatively quickly, water frequently, and feed regularly with a high nitrogen feed.

GROWING BAMBOOS

If you have limited space and are planting one of the more invasive types, it is advisable to constrict the roots. One way is to sink a much larger container into the ground and plant into this. Alternatively, contain the plant by sinking tiles, or something similar, into the ground around it. Even better, choose a non-invasive variety!

When the plant is established, after a few years, the culms can be thinned out to give a more see-through effect, and to stop overcrowding. Thinning also tends to make the culms thicker.

If you like to see more of the culms, it is advisable to remove the lateral shoots to a height of several centimetres/inches. To get really big, bamboos also need lots of water, and a good mulch of well-rotted manure.

Some of the dwarf types can be pruned back to the ground in the spring to show the new growth off at its best. Spring is also a good time to mulch bamboos with manure or compost.

Directory of exotic plants

There are many exotic plants that will thrive in the less clement conditions that prevail in the temperate regions of the world, and examples of these have been referred to in the preceding pages. This directory is intended as a more detailed guide to these plants. It has been divided into three sections. In the first section the plants are grouped according to their type, such as bamboos, or ferns, and then their genus. In the second section individual plants are organized by their genus only, with specific species covered in more detail. In both sections the emphasis is, as far as possible, on hardier plants that will thrive outdoors if extra care is taken, such as protection in winter. Finally, there is a list of houseplants that are appropriate to the exotic garden and can be placed outdoors during more temperate weather.

THE AROIDS

These are architectural, tropical and subtropical herbs. Although they are normally considered rainforest plants, many of them can withstand low temperatures with a little help during the coldest months, such as mulching with straw, or digging up the tubers and storing them in a dry, frost-free place.

ALOCASIA

Evergreen rhizomatous perennials. Commonly called the elephant's ear plant, *A. macrorrhiza* has deep-green, huge, arrow-shaped, veined leaves. Grows up to 4m (12ft) high in its native habitat but much less in temperate climes. It can take a few degrees of frost if well mulched. *A. m.* 'Jungle Gold' is smaller, with green-and-gold leaves on golden stems when mature. *A. sanderiana* is very tender, but fine in warm, sheltered spots. India, Sri Lanka.
Height Up to 4m (12ft).
Hardiness Frost tender. **US Zone** Varies according to species, but all are frost tender.
Site & Soil Very moist, humus-rich soil in sun or partial shade.

COLOCASIA

Deciduous or evergreen perennial marginals. Known as the taro, the large-leaved, and stout-stemmed *C. esculenta* is a robust and fast-growing, marginal aquatic perennial. The dark green leaves are drooping in habit. Keep

Alocasia sanderiana

as dry as possible with mulch during the winter, or dig up the tubers and store frost free.
C. e. 'Black Magic' is an absolute show-stopper, being almost black. Tropical Asia.
Height 1.5m (5ft).
Hardiness Frost tender to borderline with protection. **US Zones** 10b and 11 as year-round perennials; 8b–10a as returning perennials.
Site & Soil Very moist, humus-rich soil in partial shade.

THE BAMBOOS

Like the palms, these plants are suggestive of foreign climes, especially of the Orient. The bamboos are a large family of grasses and grass-like plants. Their waving canes and leaves catch even the lightest breeze, creating an air of mystery. Some bamboos are invasive, so you need to know the habit of the species you plant.

CHUSQUEA

Evergreen, clump-forming bamboos. *C. gigantea* has thick, yellow-green canes, with clusters of small, leafy branches providing a bottle-brush effect. Spreading, with well-spaced canes. Chile.
Height 6m (20ft).
Hardiness Hardy. **US Zone** Varies according to species.
Site & Soil Humus-rich, fertile soil in full or partial shade.

FARGESIA

Clump-forming evergreen bamboos. Most must be grown in full sun, although a few prefer dappled shade. *F. murieliae* has small leaves on arching stems, while *F. nitida* is slightly smaller, with purple streaks on the canes. Both these bamboos are ideal for small gardens. China, N.E. Himalayas.
Height 4m (12ft) or more.
Hardiness Hardy. **US Zones** 7–11.
Site & Soil Moist, fertile, humus-rich soil in sun or shade.

PHYLLOSTACHYS

Evergreen bamboos. In temperate climes these are usually fairly compact plants. *P. aurea* has bright green canes maturing to yellow. *P. nigra* is a distinct, and much sought after, plant, having canes speckled with black that over time become a burnished black. The light-green leaves make an excellent contrast. *P. n.* var. *henonsis* has glossy leaves, and bright green canes that become yellow-green when mature. *P. pubescens* produces some of the thickest canes – up to 7cm (3in) wide – and has olive-green leaves; in some areas it can get very tall. *P. vivax* also produces large lustrous green canes up to 6cm (2in). China.

Height 2–10m (6–30ft).

Hardiness Hardy. **US Zones** 7–8.

Site & Soil Fertile, humus-rich soil in full sun or dappled shade.

Sasa palmata f. *nebulosa*

PLEIOBLASTUS

Evergreen bamboos. *P. auricomus* is brilliant yellow with green stripes. An ideal plant for a container or the front of a border. *P. variegatus* is even shorter, with pale-green canes and dark green leaves with cream stripes. China, Japan.

Height Up to 1.5m (5ft) (*P. auricomus*). Up to 75cm (30in) (*P. variegatus*).

Hardiness Hardy. **US Zones** 7–11.

Site & Soil Moist, humus-rich, fertile soil in full sun or dappled shade.

SASA

Evergreen bamboos. *S. palmata* has the largest leaves of all the bamboos and a very jungle-like feel. This is a very vigorous bamboo and needs to have its roots restricted. Japan.

Height 2.5m (8ft) or more.

Hardiness Hardy. **US Zone** Varies according to species.

Site & Soil Any soil. Moist, humus-rich conditions in full sun or shade. Can be contained by a wall or tiles sunk in the ground.

THE BANANAS

These are large-leaved, tropical herbs – not trees! They are generally rapid growing and clump forming. Given the right conditions, several species will produce bananas.

ENSETE

Evergreen perennials. The Abyssinian banana or Ethiopian banana, *E. ventricosum*, has a small trunk, with paddle-shaped, olive-green leaves, up to 60cm (2ft) wide and 6m (20ft) long. *E. v.* 'Maurelii' is a dramatic, dark purple-red with intricate leaf markings. *E. v.* 'Red Stripe' has a prominent, red mid-rib. Africa and tropical Asia.

Height 6m (20ft) or more.

Hardiness Hardy to frost tender.

US Zones Varies according to species.

Site & Soil Humus-rich soil in full sun or partial shade.

Phyllostachys vivax 'Aureocaulis'

Ensete ventricosum 'Maurelii'

Musa lasiocarpa

MUSA

Evergreen perennials. For sheer hardiness the Japanese banana, *M. basjoo*, is the one to have. Protect the long stems in cooler climates to ensure that the plant grows up to a great height. It has dramatic arching leaves and is excellent when it becomes multi-stemmed. This is the plant to sit under in hot weather. *M. acuminata*, with brown blotches on its juvenile leaves, produces edible fruit. In cool locations it is best used as summer bedding, or as a container plant. With winter protection *M.* 'Orinoco' can get up to 5m (17ft) high in favourable conditions; less in cooler climates. *M.* 'Rajapuri' has deep-green leaves and needs similar conditions to *M.* 'Orinoco'. *M. lasiocarpa* (syn. *Musella lasiocarpa*) is also hardy but smaller, with yellow flowers 1m (3ft) or more long.

S. E. Asia, N. Australia and N. E. India.
Height 6m (20ft) or more.
Hardiness Frost hardy (roots only) to tender.
US Zones 5–11.
Site & Soil Any soil in sun or shade, although they respond well to high-nitrogen feeds, and the addition of organic material such as manure.

THE FERNS

This is a very large family of almost prehistoric-looking plants, many of which are evergreen. They range in size from the tall and statuesque to the diminutive.

BLECHNUM

Evergreen or semi-evergreen ferns. One of the most handsome of all ferns, *B. chilense* is a very robust, evergreen fern, with leathery, dark-green fronds, often forming a short woody trunk. It is especially attractive when planted under the tree fern *Dicksonia antarctica*. Chile, Argentina.
Height 90cm (3ft).
Hardiness Hardy. **US Zone**: 10
Site & Soil Moist, humus-rich soil in dappled to full shade.

DICKSONIA

Evergreen or semi-evergreen ferns. The woolly tree fern, *D. antarctica* is an absolute must for the exotic garden. It has a very stately trunk up to 60cm (2ft) wide, with fronds up to 3m (10ft) long, forming a massive crown. It looks even more dramatic when planted in a small glade of different-sized plants. Australia (including Tasmania).
Height Up to 6m (20ft).
Hardiness The hardiest are those from higher elevations, where they are often covered with snow in winter. In very cold weather, place straw in the crown, and bend the fronds into the middle. **US Zones** 9–11; marginal in 8.
Site & Soil Humus-rich, moist soil in dappled to full shade. Keep trunk moist at all times.

OSMUNDA

Deciduous ferns. The royal fern, *O. regalis*, has pale-green leaves that turn gold in autumn. It looks very attractive grown by streams or ponds, or in a bog garden. Europe, Asia.
Height 2m (6ft).
Hardiness Hardy. **US Zone** Varies with species.
Site & Soil Water marginal. Humus-rich soil in sun or dappled shade.

WOODWARDIA

Evergreen or deciduous ferns. The European chain fern, *Woodwardia radicans*, has arching form with fronds up to 2m (6ft) long, producing small bulbils near the tips. Eurasia, N. America.
Height: 2m (6ft).
Hardiness Hardy to −5C (40F). **US Zone** Varies according to species.
Site & Soil Damp, fertile soil in dappled shade.

Dicksonia antarctica

Cautleya spicata 'Robusta'

THE GINGERS

An absolutely essential plant in the exotic garden, gingers have fabulous-looking leaves on thrusting stalks, and flowers that can be strongly scented. The family contains the edible root ginger, *Zingiber officinale*.

ALPINIA

Evergreen perennials. The variegated ginger, *A. vittata*, has mid-green leaves with white stripes. The shell ginger, or shell lily, *A. zerumbet* 'Variegata', has dark-green foliage, striped with pale yellow. E. Asia, Australia.
Height 1–1.2m (3–4ft) or more.
Hardiness Frost tender. Plant outside in summer or grow in pots; **US Zones** 8a–11.
Site & Soil Fertile, humus-rich soil in dappled shade.

CAUTLEYA

Rhizomatous perennial. *C. spicata* is the only plant widely available in this genus. It has lance-shaped leaves, terminal, spike-like racemes, and yellow flowers with bold red bracts and sepals. The Himalayas.
Height 90cm (3ft).
Hardiness Frost hardy. **US Zones** 8–9.
Site & Soil Moist, humus-rich soil in partial shade.

CURCUMA

Rhizomatous perennials. *C. alismatifolia* is the most commonly found curcuma. It has purplish-pink bracts borne on terminal spikes. Very good for summer bedding in warmer zones. Tropical Asia, N. Australia.
Height 30cm (2ft).
Hardiness Tender. **US Zone** 9.
Site & Soil Moist, free-draining soil in dappled shade. Best grown in pots.

HEDYCHIUM

Rhizomatous perennials. Probably the best-known of all the gingers and well worth hunting out. The Kahili ginger, *H. gardnerianum*, has stout stems with fleshy leaves, 10cm (4in) wide and

Hedychium densiflorum

38cm (15in) long. The spikes are topped by sensuously scented, yellow flowers and long, orange stamens. *H. densiflorum* has smaller leaves on shorter stems. It sports tightly packed, orange, terminal flower spikes with a delicious scent. Very reliable. *H. greenii* is a stunning plant. It has largish, dark-green leaves, maroon-red underneath. In late summer it produces terminal racemes of bright orange-red flowers. Woodland areas in Asia.
Height 2–2.2m (6–7ft).
Hardiness Tender to borderline; with mulching, survives well. **US Zones** 8–11.
Site & Soil Moist, humus-rich, well-drained soil in sun or partial shade.

THE PALMS

These are essential for a really exotic look. Many can adapt well to a less than tropical climate, and they look good in winter too. The older the plant, the hardier it becomes.

BRAHEA

Single-stemmed palms. The blue hesper palm, *B. armata*, is a stunner, with pale, greyish-blue fronds. USA (S. California), Mexico.
Height 3m (10ft) or more. Slow growing.
Hardiness Moderately hardy. **US Zones** 9–11; with protection 8.
Site & Soil Ordinary, well-drained soil in a sunny, south-facing site. Protect when young, and during the coldest weather, or grow in a container and bring indoors.

BUTIA

Single-stemmed palms. *B. capitata* is a beautiful palm with arching, blue-green fronds that will eventually produce a stout trunk. Cool, dry areas in S. Brazil, Paraguay, Uruguay, Argentina.
Height 3–6m (10–20ft).
Hardiness Moderately hardy. **US Zones** 8–11.
Site & Soil Well-drained soil in a south-facing position.

CHAMAEROPS

A shrubby palm. The dwarf fan palm, *C. humilis*, is only second in hardiness to *Trachycarpus*. It can be either single stemmed or clump-forming. W. Mediterranean.

Height 2–3m (6–10ft).
Hardiness Hardy to −12°C (10°F) when established. **US Zones** 8b–11.
Site & Soil Well-drained, fertile soil in a sunny, sheltered position.

JUBAEA

A single-stemmed palm. The Chilean wine palm, *J. chilensis*, is slow growing, but eventually forms a massive trunk. The palm is topped by a crown of feathery fronds. Chile.

Height 6m (20ft) or more.
Hardiness Frost hardy. **US Zone** 7.
Site & Soil Fertile, moist, free-draining soil in full sun.

NANNORRHOPS

A fan palm. *N. ritchieana*, with its blue-grey fronds, is very ornamental and resilient to cold. It is often covered in snow for months in its native habitat, the mountains and deserts of Afghanistan and Pakistan.

Height Grows very slowly, reaching 2.5–3m (8–10ft) over many years.
Hardiness Hardy to −15°C (7°F) if kept dry.
US Zone Varies according to species.
Site & Soil Hot, dry position in full sun, or as a container plant for placing out during the summer months.

PHOENIX

Single and cluster-stemmed palms. In more temperate regions, *P. canariensis* can be either grown in a container or planted out; when outdoors, the larger the plant, the more frost resistant it becomes. Canary Islands, coastal regions of the Mediterranean.

Height 3m (10ft) or more in ideal conditions.

Hardiness Borderline. A few degrees of frost when established. **US Zones** 8–11.
Site & Soil Fertile, moist, well-drained soil in full sun, protected from cold winds. Protect for the first few years, until established.

TRACHYCARPUS

Usually single-stemmed, evergreen palms. The chusan palm, *T. fortunei*, is probably the hardiest of all the palms, and is another absolute essential in the exotic garden. The fan-shaped, mid-green fronds are up to 1m (3ft) across. Small, yellow flowers are borne in pendent panicles. *T. wagnerianus* is a miniature version. China.

Height 6m (20ft) or more.
Hardiness Once established −15°C (7°F).
US Zones 7b–11; marginal 7a.
Site & Soil Free-draining soil in sun or dappled shade. Protect from wind.

Trachycarpus wagnerianus

EXOTIC SHRUBS, CLIMBERS AND PERENNIALS

ABUTILON

Evergreen and deciduous shrubs, small trees, perennials, annuals. Some have large flowers, such as *A. x suntense* 'Violetta' with saucer-shaped purple flowers. Most have pendent flowers, with yellow petals protruding from red calyces, such as *A. megapotamicum*. Others have variegated foliage, such as *A. pictum* 'Thompsonii'. Tropical and subtropical regions of Asia, Africa, Australia, N. and S. America.

Height 2–5m (6–15ft).
Hardiness Hardy to frost tender.
US Zones 7–8.
Site & Soil Moderately fertile, well-drained soil in full sun to semi-shade.

ACANTHUS

Vigorous architectural perennials. *A. spinosus* is clump-forming, with arching, dark-green spiny leaves, and racemes of white flowers with purple, spiky bracts. *A. mollis* has deeply-lobed, dark-green leaves to 1m (3ft) long, with similar flower spikes. The Mediterranean.

Height Up to 1.5m (5ft) with flower stalk.
Hardiness Most fully hardy. **US Zones** 6–10.
Site & Soil Any soil in sun or partial shade.

AEONIUM

Evergreen perennials. All have rosette-forming foliage. Often branching, they can form small trees. One of the best plants for summer bedding, they produce yellow flowers from the centre of the rosette in pyramidal panicles. The darkest form is *A.* 'Zwartkop'. Canary Islands, the Mediterranean region.

Height 8cm–2m (3in–6ft).
Hardiness Frost tender. **US Zone** Varies according to species.
Site & Soil Thrives in gritty, fast-draining soil in full sun.

Amaranthus caudatus

ALOE

Rosetted evergreen perennials. *A. striatula* is one of the hardiest, with leaves up to 15cm (6in) long and lemon-coloured, tubular flowers. *A. aristata* is small but tough, with leaves 10cm (4in) long. All the aloes make great container plants, especially the larger ones. E. and S. regions of southern Africa, the Arabian Peninsula, Madagascar.

Height from 2.5cm (1in) to 9m (28ft).
Hardiness Tender to frost hardy.
US Zones Varies according to species.
Site & Soil Well-drained soil in full sun.

AMARANTHUS

Annuals or short-lived perennials. A favourite of the Victorians, they have upright or pendent, large, catkin-like racemes of tightly packed flowers. *A. caudatus* has light-green leaves with long, crimson-purple flowers. *A. caudatus* 'Viridis' has tassels of yellowish cream. Tropical and temperate regions of N. and S. America.

Height 60–120cm (2–4ft).
Hardiness Frost tender. **US Zones** 3–10.
Site & Soil Moist, humus-rich soil in full sun.

AMICIA

Woody-based perennials that are members of the pea family, *Leguminae*, and are grown for their foliage. The leaves, each with two pairs of leaflets, are arranged alternately on the stem. *A. zygomeris* is the only one generally available, and has mid-green leaves, 15–20cm (6–8in) long. Each leaf stalk has two pairs of heart-shaped leaflets which fold down and together in the evening. The leaf stalks arise from a pale-green stipule, flushed purple. The pea-like flowers are yellow and are borne in the autumn. The Andes, Mexico.

Height 2.2m (7ft).
Hardiness Hardy to −10°C (14°F).
US Zones Varies according to species.
Site & Soil Well-drained fertile soil in full sun.

Agave americana 'Marginata'

ARGYRANTHEMUM

Evergreen subshrubs. Produce delightful daisy flowers in a range of colours and foliage; they often flower almost continuously New cultivars are appearing all the time, but *A. foeniculaceum* is a lovely species, with finely dissected, blue-green leaves, and white flowerheads with yellow centres. *A.* 'Jamaica Primrose' has more coarsely toothed leaves on long, branching stems, bearing primrose-yellow flowerheads with a darker-yellow centre. The nearest to red is *A.* 'Rollason's Red', with bright magenta-red flowers and yellow haloes around dark centres. Loose habit. Canary Islands, Madeira.

Height 30cm–1m (1–3ft).
Hardiness Frost hardy in free-draining soil, to half hardy. **US Zone** Varies according to species.
Site & Soil Freely draining, moderately fertile soil in full sun.

ARUNDO

Evergreen perennial grasses. They have broad, linear leaves on tall canes, with bamboo-like foliage. *A. donax* is hardy, but the variegated version needs winter protection. Excellent as

AGAPANTHUS

Evergreen and deciduous perennials. They form bold clumps of arching, strap-shaped leaves. The hybrids tend to be deciduous and hardier. Grow either in the ground or in large containers in a hot, sunny position. *A. africanus* has blue flower clusters 15–30cm (6–12in). *A.* 'Snowy Owl' has white flowers. Southern Africa.

Height 60cm–1.2m (2–4ft).
Hardiness Frost hardy to tender.
US Zones 9–10.
Site & Soil Any fertile soil in full sun.

AGAVE

Monocarpic or perennial succulents. The leaves tend to be thick and leathery, with sharp spikes on the margins, and a sharp tip. Tolerates frost if kept dry through the winter, especially larger specimens. *A. americana* 'Marginata' has yellow-margined leaves that can become vast in the right conditions. C. and N. America.

Height Up to 2m (6ft) in beds, but less in pots.
Hardiness Tender to frost hardy, depending on species. **US Zone** Varies according to species.
Site & Soil Well-drained sandy soil in full sun.

large specimens at the back of the border, or as dot plants. Warm temperate parts of the northern hemisphere.
Height Up to 5m (15ft).
Hardiness Hardy to frost tender.
US Zones 6–11.
Site & Soil Moist conditions in full sun.

ASTELIA

Evergreen perennials. Form clumps of arching, linear, silvery leaves. *A. chathamica* produces long leaves of beaten silver up to 8cm (3in) wide, turning green at the base when older. A stunning plant that should be grown more often. Mountainous areas in Australasia, Hawaii, New Guinea, southern S. America.
Height Up to 2m (6ft).
Hardiness Hardy to −6°C (21°F) in a sheltered corner. **US Zone** Varies according to species.
Site & Soil Moist, fertile soil in sun or partial shade.

Astelia chathamica

AUCUBA

Evergreen shrubs. Grown for their ability to withstand drought and deep shade, and so excellent for darker corners of the garden. *A. japonica* has glossy, green leaves. Other varieties, such as A. 'Crotonifolia' and A. 'Gold Dust', have striking yellow-spotted leaves. Male plants produce red berries in the autumn. E. Asia, the Himalayas.
Height 3m (10ft).
Hardiness Hardy. **US Zones** 7–10.
Site & Soil Sun to shade in any soil.

BEGONIA

Annuals, perennials, shrubs, and climbers. Many of the tuberous hybrids that produce large flowers make excellent bedding or container plants. *B. fuchsioides* is a shrub-like begonia with shiny green leaves and pink, fuchsia-like flowers. *B. grandis* subsp. *evensiana* is probably the hardiest begonia. Its typical begonia leaves are green with red veins. Pendent flowers are pink or white. Many of the traditional houseplant types, such as *B.* x *argenteoguttata*, can stand out or be temporarily bedded out in summer. Widespread in tropical and subtropical regions.
Height 20–90cm (8in–3ft)
Hardiness Most are frost tender, a few are half-hardy. **US Zone** 10.
Site & Soil Fertile, moist, humus-rich, well-drained, neutral to slightly acid, in dappled shade.

BERGENIA

Evergreen perennials. Although not tropical in nature, they have a tropical appearance. There are many varieties. *B. cordifolia* is a clump-forming perennial, with rounded to heart-shaped leaves tinted purple in winter; it bears pink flowers on red stems in late winter to early spring. *B. ciliata* has large, broadly ovate, hairy, mid-green leaves that appear after the flowers, which are produced in spring and are pinkish-white. In frosty areas leaves die back in winter. Damp

woodlands in C. and E. Asia.
Height 20–60cm (8in–2ft).
Hardiness Hardy to frost tender. **US Zone** 4.
Site & Soil Moist, ordinary to poor soil in sun or shade.

BESCHORNERIA

Perennial succulents. Clump-forming rosettes of soft, leathery, glaucous, grey-green leaves. *B. yuccoides* produces pinnacles up to 1.5m (5ft) or more long, with red bracts at the ends, and yellow to intense green flowers. Mexico.
Height 1.5m (5ft) or more.
Hardiness Will take a few degrees of frost, but more with protection. **US Zone** Varies according to species.
Site & Soil Well-drained, humus-rich soil in full sun.

BOUGAINVILLEA

Evergreen trees and shrubs, deciduous and evergreen climbers. Grown not for their small

Bougainvillea 'Jennifer Fernie'

Brugmansia x *candida* 'Knightii'

insignificant flowers but for the surrounding petal-like bracts that come in a large range of colours. They will survive short periods down to 0°C (32°F) if kept dry in winter, when they will probably drop their leaves. Grown up a wall or over a pergola they look superb. Otherwise, in cooler temperate regions, keep as a glasshouse or conservatory plant, or stand out during the warmer summer months. The following species are borderline hardy: *B.* 'Jennifer Fernie', with white, yellow-veined bracts. *B. glabra*, especially vigorous, with white to magenta flora bracts, borne mainly in summer and autumn. *B.* 'Mary Palmer', vigorous, with pink to white or bicolour bracts. *B.* 'Scarlett O'Hara', vigorous, with stunning scarlet-cerise bracts. Tropical and subtropical S. America.
Height 5–12m (15–40ft).
Hardiness Half-hardy to frost tender.
US Zone 10.
Site & Soil Fertile, well-drained soil in full sun.

BRUGMANSIA

Evergreen shrubs and trees. Grown either as a bush, or on a single stem so that you can gaze up into the large, intensely scented flowers. The trumpets are up to 30cm (12ins) long. Grown either in large pots or in the ground during the summer months. These luscious plants are voracious feeders and drinkers. *B.* x *candida* 'Nightii' has large, white or soft yellow, ageing to white, trumpet flowers that are scented at night. *B.* 'Variegata Sunset' has pale-yellow flowers with variegated leaves. S. America to southern USA.
Height Up to 5m (15ft).
Hardiness Frost tender.
US Zones 9b as a returning perennial, 10–11 as a permanent plant.
Site & Soil Humus-rich, moist soil in full sun.

CAMPSIS

Deciduous climber. Funnel-shaped flowers from summer to autumn. The common trumpet creeper, *C. radicans*, has intense, orange-red flowers. *C.* x *tagliabuana* 'Madame Galen' has flowers 11cm (4in) long x 8cm (3in) wide, borne in clusters. One of the best exotic climbers for cool climates. N. America and China.
Height 10m (30ft) or more.
Hardiness Hardy. **US Zone** 5.
Site & Soil Moderately fertile soil. Best grown against a south-facing wall.

Campsis radicans

Canna 'Roi Soleil'

CANNA

Rhizomatous herbaceous perennial. Flamboyant flowers on huge, exotic, banana-like leaves. The foliage is usually green or bronze, although *C.* 'Striata' is green with yellow veins, and sports an orange, gladiolus-like flower. *C.* 'Durban' is another stunner, with dark, purple-red leaves and pink veins. *C.* 'King Humbert' has bronze leaves, and deep-red flowers. *C.* 'Picasso' has green leaves, and yellow flowers faintly spotted red. Asia and tropical N. and S. America.
Height 60cm–2m (2–6ft).
Hardiness Frost tender, but can be left in the ground if well mulched. **US Zones** 8–10.
Site & Soil Humus-rich, moist soil in full light.

CITRUS

Evergreen trees and shrubs. An essential plant for the Mediterranean feel. Glossy, green leaves that are pungent if squeezed, and often intensely scented, white flowers. There are many varieties of lemon, orange, mandarin, tangerine, and lime. S. E. Asia.

Height Up to 12m (40ft), but far less when grown in pots.

Hardiness 0°C (32°F) for short periods only.

US Zones 7–8.

Site & Soil Unless mild winters, best grown in a pot in well-drained soil.

CLEMATIS

Evergreen or deciduous climbers and herbaceous perennials. Many varieties of clematis fit well in the exotic garden, but one of the best is the vigorous *Clematis armandii*, which has large, luscious, lanceolate-pointed, evergreen leaves. Flowers in the spring are up to 5cm (2in) across and heavily scented. *C. a.* 'Apple Blossom' has pink-tinged white blooms. *C.* 'Alba Luxurians' is late-flowering, and has mid-green foliage and small, open, bell-shaped flowers, 5–7cm (2–3ins) across, that are white with irregular, green petal tips. Northern and southern hemispheres.

Height 3–5m (10–15ft).

Hardiness Fairly hardy. **US Zones** 5–9.

Site & Soil Fertile, free-draining soil in sun or partial shade.

CORDYLINE

Evergreen shrubs or tree-like perennials. With arching, tufted leaves and lily-scented flowers. Resembling palm trees, but faster growing, the New Zealand cabbage palm, *C. australis*, is the hardiest, while *C. a.* 'Purpurea', with deep-purple leaves, is less so. There are several varieties, including the stunning *C. a.* 'Albertii', with red mid-rib and cream-pink stripes. S.E. Asia, the Pacific, Australasia.

Height 3–10m (10–30ft).

Hardiness Frost tender to −7°C (19°F) for short periods. Will reshoot from base if frozen.

US Zones Varies according to species.

Site & Soil Fertile soil in sun or partial shade.

CYNARA

Clump-forming perennials. They have large, spiky, silvery-grey leaves, topped in summer with purple, artichoke-like fluorides. *C. cardunculus*, cardoon, is a massive plant for the back of the border. Stake well as it can flop when in full bloom. N.W. Africa, Canary Islands, the Mediterranean.

Height 1.5–2m (5–6ft).

Hardiness Hardy. **US Zones** 6–10.

Site & Soil Fertile, free-draining soil in sun.

CYPERUS

Grass-like annuals and evergreen rhizomatous perennials. Like boggy conditions, but will grow in dryer situations if watered regularly. Grows well outside in warmer months in temperate regions. Lift before the first frosts. *C. papyrus* has tall, triangular stems with large, compound, ray-like threads. *C. alternifolius* is much smaller. *C. eragrostis* can take dryer conditions and tolerates frost. Subtropical and tropical areas.

Cyperus papyrus

Dahlia 'David Howard'

Height 45cm–2m (18in–6ft).

Hardiness Hardy to tender. **US Zones** Varies according to species; *C. alternifolius* 10.

Site & Soil Very moist, humus-rich soil in sun or partial shade.

DAHLIA

Tuberous-rooted perennials. Now back in popularity, especially the dark-leaved forms such as *D.* 'Bishop of Llandaff', an old cultivar with black-red leaves, and single, red flowers, with a centre that turns from maroon to yellow. *D.* 'Bednall Beauty' is a similar colour, but shorter and self supporting. *D.* 'Yellow Hammer' is bronze-leaved, with creamy yellow flowers. *D.* 'David Howard' has rich yellow flowers with orange centres. Asia and tropical N. and S. America.

Height 60cm–3m (2–10ft).

Hardiness The roots are hardy if mulched, otherwise tender. **US Zone** 10.

Site & Soil Humus-rich, moist soil in full sun.

DICLIPTERA

Annuals, evergreen subshrubs, perennials, and climbers. *D. suberecta* is an arching subshrub with slender stems, and dull, mid-green leaves covered in fine, velvet-like hairs. The flowers are tubular in shape, and are orange-red, borne in terminal bunches. This is a delightful plant that should be grown more often. Uruguay.

Height 60cm (2ft).

Hardiness Frost tender, but roots survive well if mulched in the autumn.

US Zone Varies according to species.

Site & Soil Moderately fertile soil in sun or dappled shade.

ERYTHRINA

Deciduous or evergreen shrubs, subshrubs, trees, and climbers. Cock's comb, *E. crista-galli* is a most unusual plant: an open, deciduous tree in warmer climates, but treated as a woody-based perennial in temperate regions. The branches bear sharp spines and leathery mid-green leaves. Exotic, red, pea-like flowers 5–6cm (2–2⅜in) long are borne on racemes 30–60cm

Erythrina crista-galli

Eucomis bicolor

(1–2ft) or more long from summer to autumn. E. Bolivia to Argentina.

Height 1.5–2.5m (5–8ft) as perennial.

Hardiness The roots frost hardy to −10°C (14°F) if heavily mulched. **US Zones** Hardy as a tree in 9b–11 and as a perennial shrub in 8–9a.

Site & Soil Fertile, well-drained soil in full sun.

EUCOMIS

Bulbous perennials. Resembling a pineapple. *E. bicolor* produces semi-erect, strap-shaped leaves. The maroon-stemmed racemes bear pale-green flowers. *E. comosa* is similar, but has much taller flowers with a greenish spike which has white flowers with purple tepal margins and ovaries. *E. punctata* has striking, purple racemes. South Africa and tropical southern Africa.

Height 30–75cm (12–30in).

Hardiness Borderline, but will survive if mulched well. **US Zones** 8–10.

Site & Soil Fertile, well-drained soil in full sun.

EUPHORBIA

Annuals, biennals, evergreen, semi-evergreen, or herbaceous perennials. A very large family, many of which fit well into the exotic garden. *E. characias* subsp. *wulfenii* is clump-forming, with erect, purple-tinted stems, and grey-green leaves. In spring, dense, cylindrical flowerheads are produced in pale lemon-green. *E. dulcis* 'Chameleon' is much smaller and deciduous. It has pointed, oblong leaves of deep purple. In autumn the leaves turn from red to gold. *E. griffithii* is another deciduous plant, with reddish-green stems when young and mid-green leaves. In early summer, the tops of the stems turn a fiery orange-red. *E. g.* 'Dixter' is a very good variety. *E. mellifera* is an evergreen shrub with long, straight stems, sporting mid-green, oblong, pointed leaves. In late spring it has honey-scented flowers. Temperate, subtropical, and tropical regions worldwide.

Height 30cm–2m (1–6ft).

Hardiness Frost hardy to tender.

US Zones 3–10.

Site & Soil Well-drained soil in full sun.

FARFUGIUM

Rhizomatous evergreen perennials. Grown for its fabulous foliage with large leathery leaves. *F. japonicum* 'Aureomaculatum' has almost unnatural, acid-like splashes on a dark-green background. *F. j.* 'Argentium' (syn. *Ligularia tussilaginea*) has shiny leaves, 15–30cm (6–12in), and is variegated with irregular, creamy-white margins. East Asia.

Height 60cm (2ft).

Hardiness Frost hardy. **US Zones** 4–8.

Site & Soil Moist, well-drained soil in partial shade.

FATSIA

Evergreen shrubs. A very good evergreen plant for an exotic touch. *F. japonica* has large, palmate-lobed, green leaves with pale-yellow veins. In the

Euphorbia characias subsp. *wulfenii*

autumn, creamy-coloured umbels appear on long stems. E. Asia.

Height 1.5–4m (5–12ft).

Hardiness Hardy to half-hardy. **US Zones** 7–9.

Site & Soil Fertile, well-drained soil, and protect from wind.

GERBERA

Perennials. Spreading rosettes of lobed, or pinnate, toothed leaves, with long-lasting, solitary single or double flowers, similar to those of the daisy, in a wide range of colours. Can be either grown in pots or bedded out in the summer. G. 'Californian Giants' has single flowers in shades of yellow, orange, red, pink, and apricot. Africa (except for N. Africa), Asia.

Height 30–45cm (12–18in).

Hardiness Half-hardy to frost tender. **US Zone** 8.

Site & Soil Moderately fertile, well-drained soil in full sun.

GUNNERA

Rhizomatous, herbaceious or evergreen perennials. Renowned for their massive and handsome leaves. G. manicata has prominently veined, and deeply-toothed, deep-green leaves up to 2m (6ft) wide. A marginal water plant, it can also be grown in large containers, although it then produces smaller leaves. Australasia, S. America, southern Africa.

Height 2.5m (8ft) or more.

Hardiness Hardy, but cover crown with old leaves in winter. **US Zones** 7–10.

Site & Soil Humus-rich soil in sun or dappled shade.

HEMEROCALLIS

The flowers only open for one day, but a succession can be had for weeks. They are edible, and look great in salads. There are many varieties, but H. 'Burning Daylight', with its yellow-orange flowers, is a stunner. For scent, the smaller, yellow-flowered H. lilioasphodelus is recommended. Japan, Korea, China.

Height Up to 75cm (30in).

Hardiness Hardy. **US Zones** 6–7.

Site & Soil Fertile, free-draining soil in full sun.

HOSTA

Mostly clump-forming perennials. Among the all-time favourite plants. One of the largest is H. sieboldiana, with its large, glaucous, blue-grey leaves. An excellent, yellow-gold-leaved variety is H. 'Sum and Substance', with leaves at least 30cm (12in) across when well fed. China, Korea, E. Russia.

Height Up to 75cm (30in).

Hardiness Hardy. **US Zones** 3–9.

Site & Soil Fertile, moist soil in dappled shade.

HUMULUS

Herbaceous perennials. Rapid-growing climber. The female inflorescences (hops) are traditionally used for making beer hops. H. lupulus 'Aureus' has golden-yellow, palmate leaves, and looks attractive even in dull weather. Northern temperate regions.

Height 6m (20ft) or more.

Hardiness Hardy. **US Zones** 3–9.

Site & Soil Moist, humus-rich soil in sun or partial shade.

IPOMOEA

Annuals and perennials, many of which are trailers or climbers. Species range from the popular morning glory, the fast-growing annual I. tricolor 'Heavenly Blue', which has bright-blue flowers with white throats, to the perennial I. indica, with its heart-shaped leaves, and abundant, rich-purple, funnel-shaped flowers. I. coccinea, far more diminutive, has toothed leaves and red flowers, while I. lobata has racemes of narrow, tubular flowers, fading from orange and yellow to white. Temperate regions everywhere.

Height 2–5m (6–15ft).

Hardiness Frost tender. **US Zone** 10.

Site & Soil Moderately fertile soil in full sun.

Ipomoea lobata

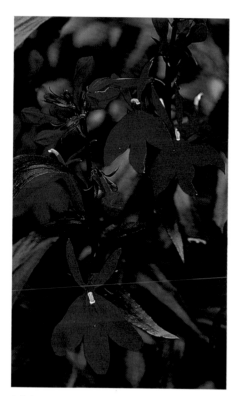

Lobelia cardinalis

LOBELIA

Annuals, perennials, and shrubs. Interesting species to be recommended for the exotic garden include *L. tupa*, a tall, upright, clump-forming perennial, with light, grey-green, lance-shaped leaves. Two-lipped, tubular, brick-red flowers are produced on terminal spikes. *L. cardinalis* is a short-lived, clump-forming perennial, with dark, purple-black leaves. The flowers are a stunning contrast in vivid scarlet. Tropical and temperate areas worldwide, especially the Americas.

Height 15cm–2m (6in–6ft).

Hardiness Hardy to frost tender.

US Zones Varies according to species.

Site & Soil Fertile, moist soil in sun or dappled shade.

LYSICHTON

Marginal, aquatic perennials. In spring an elongated, bright-yellow spathe is thrust up from the ground, followed by ovate-oblong, leathery, bright-green leaves that look like a giant cos lettuce. Skunk cabbage, *L. americanus*, is widely available. The whole plant gives off a musky scent. N. E. Asia, W. and N. America.

Height 1m (3ft).

Hardiness Hardy. **US Zones** 4–9.

Site & Soil Humus-rich soil in water margin. Dappled light.

IRESINE

Evergreen erect or climbing perennials, annuals, and subshrubs. These are stunningly coloured foliage plants that make excellent bedding during the summer months. The beefsteak plant, *I. herbstii*, is an erect bush with small, round, purple leaves. *I. h.* 'Aureoreticulata' has red stems with green leaves, veined cream-yellow. *I. h.* 'Brilliantissima', with its vivid (almost day-glo) magenta leaves and stems, is irresistible. *I.* 'Formosa' has yellow leaves veined in crimson. *I. lindenii* has narrow, pointed, dark, reddish-purple leaves. S. America, Australia.

Height 60cm (2ft) or more.

Hardiness Tender. **US Zones** 10–11 as permanent perennials; 9b as a returning perennial.

Site & Soil Moist, fertile, well-drained soil in full sun.

Magnolia grandiflora 'Goliath'

Lysichton americanus

MAGNOLIA

Deciduous and evergreen trees and shrubs. The evergreen varieties are the best to grow for an exotic effect. *M. hypoleuca*, the Japanese big-leaf magnolia, has mid-green leaves, 40cm (16in) long, and creamy white, highly scented flowers. *M. grandiflora* 'Goliath' has large, long, shiny, leathery leaves that are a soft, velvety brown on the underside. The creamy-white flowers are huge – 20–30cm (8–12in) across. It can be trained against a wall. These plants are very prehistoric looking! From the Himalayas to E. and S. E. Asia, and from eastern N. America to tropical N. and S. America.

Height 6–18m (20–60ft).

Hardiness Hardy. **US Zones** 4–7.

Site & Soil Moist, humus-rich, preferably acid soil in sun or partial shade. They need protecting from the wind.

Melianthus major

MELIANTHUS

Evergreen shrubs. A very desirable foliage plant for an exotic look. The deeply lobed and serrated leaves are glaucous, grey-green, and smell of peanuts. *M. major* looks great planted with cannas. Mulch around the stems in winter and cut to the ground in spring. Southern Africa.
Height 2–3m (6–9ft).
Hardiness Borderline, but with protection the roots are hardy.
US Zones Varies according to species.
Site & Soil Moist, well-drained soil, full sun.

PASSIFLORA

Mostly evergreen climbers with breathtaking flowers. *P. caerulea* is one of the hardiest and bears star-shaped, white or pink-tinged flowers, with purple-blue and white-zoned coronas. The hardy *P. incata* has 3–5 lobed leaves and white to pale-purple, bowl-shaped flowers 8cm (3in) in diameter, followed by yellow, egg-shaped fruit. *P. quadrangularis*, although not hardy, can be grown in containers for the summer. It has nodding, fragrant red flowers, with a massive corona of wavy filaments, banded purple and white. New Zealand, Australia, the Pacific Islands, tropical Asia, N., C. and S. America.
Height 10m (30ft) or more.
Hardiness Fully hardy to frost tender.
US Zones Varies according to species; *P. caerulea* 7–10.
Site & Soil Moist, well-drained soil in sun or partial shade.

PELARGONIUM

Mainly evergreen perennials, succulents, subshrubs, and shrubs. Not to be confused with geraniums. These make excellent plants for the warmer months, from the scented to the showy, brash types. Zonal types such as *P.* 'Paul Crampel' can become large either grown in a container or against a wall and will give a stunning effect.

Passiflora quadrangularis

Ricinus communis 'Carmencita'

P. 'Mrs Quilter' is a zonal pelargonium, with gold leaves with bronze zones, and clusters of pink flowers. South Africa.
Height 30cm–3m (12in–9ft).
Hardiness Frost tender. **US Zones** 9–10.
Site & Soil Well-drained soil in full sun.

RICINUS

Evergreen shrubs. Fast-growing plants grown as annuals in frost-prone areas. In one season these dramatic plants can get very large, with *R. communis* 'Zanzibarensis' producing leaves up to 60cm (2ft) wide. *R. c.* 'Carmencita' sports dark-bronze foliage with red female flowers. N.E. Africa to W. Asia.
Height 2–3m (6–9ft).
Hardiness Frost tender. **US Zones** 8–10.
Site & Soil Humus-rich, free-draining soil in full sun.

SENECIO

Annuals, biennials, herbaceous perennials, climbers, shrubs, succulents, and small trees. *S. confusus* is a moderately shrubby, sprawling, evergreen climber with mid-green, arrow-shaped leaves. The scented flowerheads are daisy-like, orange turning red, borne on terminal bunches. *S. grandifolius* has mid-green, coarsely-toothed leaves 20–45cm (8–18in) long. Domed, multiple, yellow flowerheads are produced in winter. Worldwide. *S. confusus* Mexico to Honduras; *S. grandifolius* Mexico.
Height 3m (10ft) or more.
Hardiness Tender. **US Zones** 10b–11 as permanent perennials; 9b–10a as returning perennials.
Site & Soil Fertile, well-drained soil in partial shade. The above species are best grown in containers and placed outside during the warmer months.

SOLANUM

Annuals, biennials, herbaceous perennials, and evergreen, semi-evergreen and deciduous shrubs, trees, and climbers. *S. crispum* is a fast-growing, scrambling plant with dark-green leaves up to 12cm (5in) long. In summer, fragrant, purple-blue flowers are produced in terminal bunches, 15cm (6in) across. *S. c.* 'Glasnevin' has deeper purple-blue flowers. *S. jasminoides* has a similar habit, but much smaller, glossy, dark-green leaves. *S. laciniatum* is a vigorous evergreen shrub, with lance-shaped leaves up to 20cm (8in) long. The dark-blue flowers are 5cm (2in) across, and are followed by green fruit that turns bright orange in the autumn. S. America, Australia, New Zealand.
Height 2–6m (6–20ft).
Hardiness Frost hardy to frost tender. *S. laciniatum* can be grown as an annual in cooler areas. **US Zones** 8–11.
Site & Soil Moderately fertile, well-drained soil in full sun.

Solanum crispum 'Glasnevin'

SOLENOSTEMON

Evergreen subshrubby perennials. Formerly known as *Coleus*. This fast-growing foliage plant comes in every colour imaginable, and the combinations are endless. A taster might be *S.* 'Black Prince', with almost black leaves, making an excellent contrast to *S.* 'Lemon Dash' with its stunning lemon leaves. Tropical Africa, Asia.
Height 90cm (3ft).
Hardiness Tender. Bed out in the summer months or in pots. **US Zones** 10–11 as permanent perennials; marginal in 9.
Site & Soil Humus-rich, fertile, well-drained soil in full sun.

SPARRMANNIA

Evergreen shrubs and small trees. It is normally considered a houseplant, but is well worth

growing outside. It has a branching habit with large, light-green leaves. South Africa.
Height 3m (10ft).
Hardiness Borderline. Roots will survive light frost if well mulched; otherwise bed out in the summer or grow in a large container.
US Zone Varies according to species.
Site & Soil Fertile, well-drained soil in sun or dappled shade.

STRELITZIA

Clump-forming, evergreen perennials. The crane flower, *S. reginae*, has wide, lance-shaped leaves, up to 50cm (20in) long and rounded at the base. From winter to spring it produces an exotic, green spathe, with an orange-flushed edge and upright orange flowers. *S. nicolai* has much larger leaves, and in the spring produces brownish-red spathes with white flowers. These plants are not hardy, but are well worth growing outside for the foliage, and inside in the winter for their tropical flowers. South Africa.
Height Up to 2m (6ft), but far less in pots.
Hardiness Frost tender. **US Zones** Varies according to species.
Site & Soil Fertile, moist, well-drained soil in sun or dappled shade. Grown in a container, they flower more reliably when potbound.

THUNBERGIA

Annuals, evergreen perennials and twining climbers. Grown mostly for their showy trumpet-shaped flowers. *T. alata*, black-eyed Susan, is a perennial twining climber usually grown as an annual. Mid-green, arrow-shaped leaves, and single flowers in orange, yellow, or white with chocolate eyes. Madagascar, tropical regions of Asia, southern Africa.
Height 2–6m (6–20ft).
Hardiness Frost tender. **US Zones** Varies according to species.
Site & Soil Moist, well-drained soil in sun or shade.

Tithonia rotundifolia 'Goldfinger'

during the summer. *T. zebrina* is a trailing plant whose blue-green leaves have striped silver-and-purple undersides. N.C., and S.America.

Height Either trailing or up to 90cm (3ft).

Hardiness Frost tender to hardy.

US Zones 5–10.

Site & Soil Moist, fertile and well drained in full sun or dappled shade.

ZANTEDESCHIA

Perennials. Arum lilies are moisture-loving plants with unusual flowers. *Z. aethiopica* 'Crowborough' is the hardiest, with mid-green, arrow-shaped leaves. During the summer it produces pure-white spathes with yellow central spadices. *Z. a.* 'Green Goddess' has larger leaves, with white-flushed, green-edged spathes. Southern and eastern Africa.

Height 60cm (2ft).

Hardiness Borderline, but the roots overwinter well with protection.

US Zones 8–11; marginal in 7.

Site & Soil Grow as a pond or bog plant, or in humus-rich, moist soil in sun or dappled shade.

Zantedeschia aethiopica 'Crowborough'

TITHONIA

Annuals, perennials, and shrubs. The Mexican sunflower, *T. rotundifolia*, is a robust, branching annual with bright-orange flowers, 8cm (3in) across, on long, hollow tubes. *T. r.* 'Goldfinger' is more compact with orange flowers. *T. r.* 'Torch' has orange-red flowers. Mexico, C. America.

Height 75cm–2m (30in–6ft).

Hardiness Frost tender. **US Zones** 3–10.

Site & Soil Fertile, well-drained soil in full sun.

TRADESCANTIA

Evergreen perennials including trailing, clump-forming, and creeping species. Green-, often purple-tinted leaves to 35cm (14in) long, with three-petalled flowers in a range of colours. Usually grown as houseplants, but many are worth trying as groundcover in the garden

HOUSEPLANTS FOR THE EXOTIC GARDEN

The following are some of the houseplants that can safely be placed outside during the warmer summer months. There are obviously many more worth trying. Remember that these are tender plants and they will be not be able to cope with severe weather conditions.

Begonia	*Furcraea*	*Plectranthus*
Caladium	*Gloriosa*	*Sansevieria*
Calathea	*Guzmania*	*Streptocarpus*
Chlorophytum	*Hypoestes*	*Tillandsia*
Codiaeum	*Lampranthus*	*Tradescantia*
Crassula	*Lantana*	*Vriesea*
Croton	*Mirabilis*	
Dracaena	*Monstera*	
Ficus	*Platycerium*	

Index

Page numbers in *italics* refer to picture captions.

Acknowledgments

Publisher's Acknowledgments

Jonathan Buckley 38-39, 53 bottom, 111 top; David Clarke 6–7, 90-91; Eric Crichton 49, 106 bottom, 115 bottom; Garden Picture Library/Mark Bolton 106 top/Chris Burrows 112 top/Brian Carter 79; top/Christi Carter 24/Michael Diggin 35/John Glover 110 top left/Michael Howes; 73/Howard Rice 109 bottom right/Juliette Wade 14–15 centre/Mel Watson 50/Didier; Willery 65 left; Garden Exposure/Derek Harris 44–5, 68; Will Giles 8, 9, 10, 10–11 centre, 12, 13, 14 left, 16–17 centre, 18, 20–1, 22, 23, 26, 27, 28, 32–33, 34, 40, 42, 43 top, 43 bottom, 51, 53 top, 58, 61 top, 66–7 centre, 70, 71, 77, 78, 82 top, 82–3 centre, 104 bottom right, 105 top, 112 bottom; Mick Hales 19, 25, 86–7 centre; Harpur Garden Library/Jerry Harpur 1/Marcus Harpur 84, 113 bottom, 116, 117; Howard Rice 108 top left, 110 bottom; Andrew Lawson Photography 17 right, 29, 103, 104 top, 109 bottom left, 111; bottom, 115 top left, 115 top right; Beth Chatto Gardens, Essex 52, 79 bottom; Heligan Manor Gardens 56–7; Marianne Majerus endpapers, 41, 48 top, 54 top, 54 bottom, 55, 69, 72, 88–9 centre, 110 top right, 113 top/Designer: Will Giles 2/Designer: Martin Gibbons 61 bottom/The Old Vicarage, East Ruston, Norfolk 4–5; David Markson 48 bottom; Mise au Point Jardin Exotique de Roscoff, France 89 bottom centre right; Octopus Publishing Group Ltd/Sue Atkinson 31, 60; Howard Rice 37 top, 37 bottom, 46 centre, 47 right, 59, 64, 65 right, 66, 80, 86 left, 104 bottom left, 105 bottom, 107, 114 bottom; Clive Nichols Garden Pictures 114 top left, 114 top right/Beth Chatto Garden, Essex 77 bottom, 81/La Mortola Garden 62–3; Jerry Pavia 30, 74–5; Franca Speranza/Renato Valterza 36; Derek St Romaine 108 right.

The publishers would also like to thank Casey Horton and Arlene Sobel for their editorial help.

Author's Acknowledgments

I wish to thank Jane Green, Nick Bartlett and Andrew Mott for their invaluable help in making my exotic garden look the way it is today. Also, Ian Cook for being the main supplier of canna over the years for the garden from his National Collection. A big thank you to the staff at Mitchell Beazley for guiding me through this, my first book. Finally, many thanks to Phil Collin for creating a fantastic website: www.exoticgarden.com.

Will Giles, October 1999.